Alfred's

Classroom

Music for Little Mozarts

10 Sequential Lessons for ages 4–6

Singing, Listening, Movement and Rhythm Activities to Bring Out the Music in Every Young Child

CD enclosed

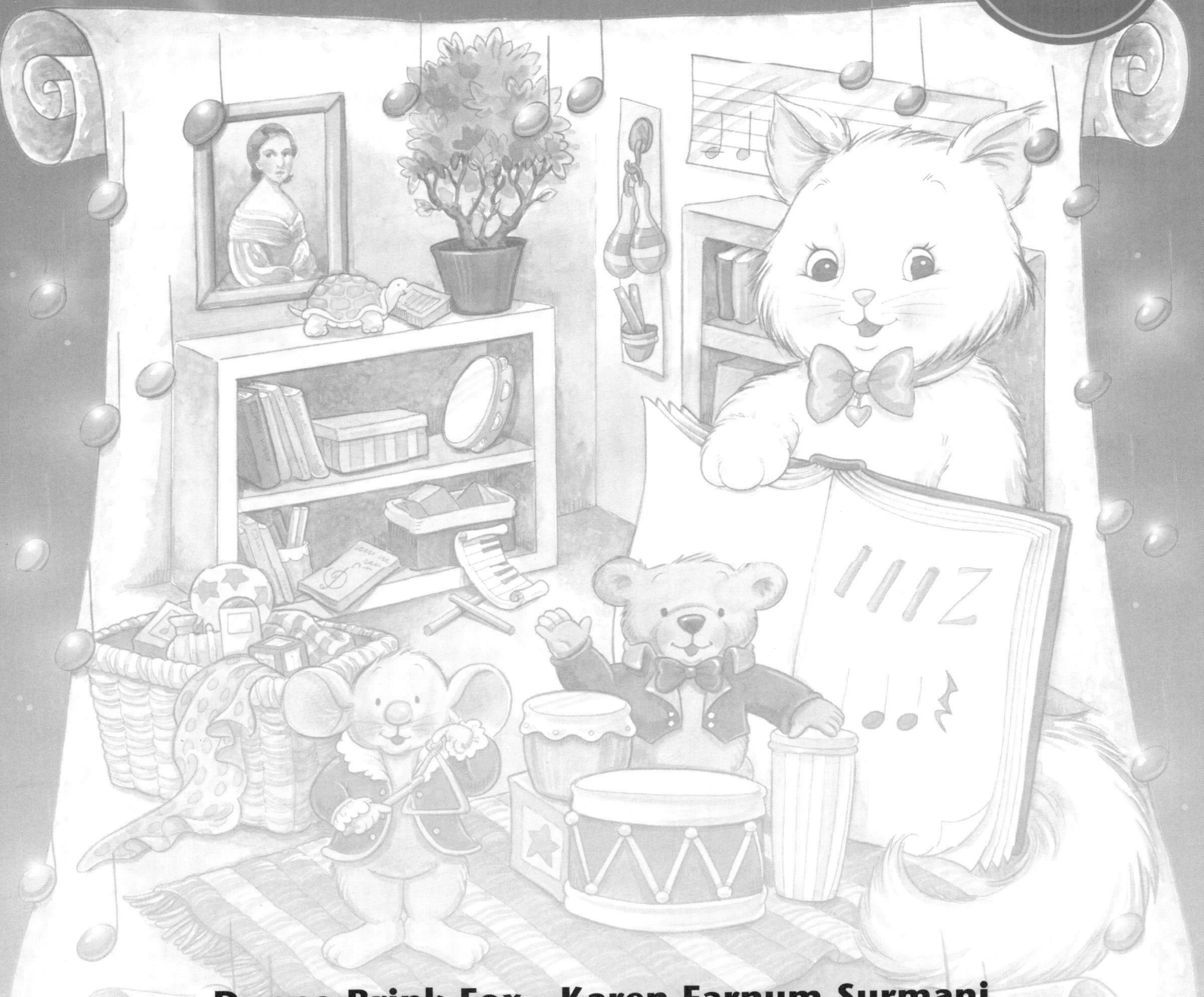

Donna Brink Fox · Karen Farnum Surmani
Christine H. Barden · Gayle Kowalchyk · E. L. Lancaster

Cover illustration and interior art by Christine Finn

Alfred Music Publishing Co., Inc.
16320 Roscoe Blvd., Suite 100
P.O. Box 10003
Van Nuys, CA 91410-0003

ISBN-10: 0-7390-3511-8
ISBN-13: 978-0-7390-3511-5

alfred.com

Table of Contents

Preliminary Information

About Classroom Music for Little Mozarts

The *Classroom Music for Little Mozarts* series was written to provide appropriate classroom music instruction for four-, five-, and six-year olds. It can be taught by music teachers or early childhood classroom teachers with minimal music backgrounds. Book 1 is the first of three books that guide the teacher and the children through a comprehensive approach to music learning that includes singing, listening, structured and expressive movement, rhythm activities, playing classroom instruments, and visual representations of notation. Each of the three books in the series includes ten lessons with the three books providing a comprehensive curriculum for a full year of music instruction. The musical experiences in *Classroom Music for Little Mozarts* address the National Standards for Music Education* for young children, and also offer opportunities to link music to other curriculum areas in the classroom. The classroom program centers around the adventures of Beethoven Bear and Mozart Mouse, characters who live in an early childhood classroom, as they learn about music.

Note: The lessons in *Classroom Music for Little Mozarts* were adapted from *Music for Little Mozarts,* an innovative piano series for young children.

*See Appendix G, page 129, and Appendix H, page 130.

To the Teacher

The materials in this book are divided into three parts: 1) Preliminary Information; 2) Classroom Lesson Plans; and 3) Support Materials.

Preliminary Information (pages 4–15): This section provides background material to serve as an aid to planning for lessons. It includes general information on teaching music to four-, five-, and six-year olds and details about teaching the *Classroom Music for Little Mozarts* curriculum.

Classroom Lesson Plans (pages 16–75): The ten lesson plans, designed for a classroom lesson of 30–45 minutes, follow. Each lesson plan consists of four parts: 1) a list of teaching materials needed for the lesson; 2) a lesson overview—a brief summary of what is included in the lesson; 3) a detailed lesson plan, including step-by-step instructions for teaching the curriculum; and 4) suggestions to connect the lesson to activities that children can pursue either independently or with a teacher in a classroom Music Center.

Support Materials (pages 76–136): The appendices include

- information regarding student assessment,
- a track listing for the compact disc,
- a complete copy of the story,
- copies of pages from the Big Music Book,
- reproducible coloring pages,
- vocal/piano arrangements of all the songs included on the CD,
- a list of the National Standards for Music Education, and
- indexes to aid with locating materials in the course.

Complete List of Materials Needed to Teach *Classroom Music for Little Mozarts,* Level 1:

Curriculum Book 1 with CD (22023)
Big Music Book 1 (23804)
Mozart Mouse Plush Animal (14653)
Beethoven Bear Plush Animal (14654)
Clara Schumann-Cat Plush Animal (19767)
CD player
Crayons for each student

Classroom Instruments: *Please order from your favorite music dealer. If you are having difficulty obtaining these and would like a referral to a music dealer in your area, please visit our website at www.alfred.com or call (818) 892-2452.*

1 xylophone and mallet
shakers (1 for each student)
rhythm sticks (1 pair for each student)

The Importance of Early Childhood Music

Educators and psychologists from the beginning of the twentieth century to the present have attested to the value of music study on the development of the child. According to Jean Piaget (1896–1980), the noted Swiss psychologist, a child's early years are the optimum period for intellectual development. He believed that children and adults think in different ways. During the "pre-operational" learning stage (ages 2–7), children begin to think and react through symbols (language, drama, drawings and dreams). This stage is perfect for starting the process of learning music.

Jerome Bruner (b. 1915), an important American cognitive psychologist, believes that the foundations of any subject can be taught to anybody at any age. In his theories, he places great emphasis on teaching the structure of the subject. He developed a spiral curriculum where general principles are presented and applied to various learning situations in ever-increasing complexity. Learning should be structured to serve the future.

The study of music at a young age is supported by the humanist theories of Abraham Maslow (1908–1970) and leads to a fully realized person (self-actualized). Harvard psychologist Howard Gardner (b. 1943) sets forth a theory that some children seem to "think musically" at a very young age. These children represent a small percentage of our society, but Gardner suggests that the numbers might increase if music were taught at a young age. Young children have the ability to understand music intuitively through performance and/or composition. In addition, they seem to have a genetic predisposition to hear, remember and produce musical patterns regardless of whether or not they are products of musical environments.[1]

Several recent studies show improved spatial-temporal task scores and pattern-recognition scores for children in different age groups who had received piano instruction as compared to the same-age control groups without piano instruction. These studies report that piano instruction is far superior to computer instruction in enhancing a child's abstract reasoning skills necessary for learning science and math. In research reported by Frances Rauscher (University of Wisconsin, Oshkosh) and associates in the February 1997 issue of ***Neurological Research***, children who had received music instruction (including keyboard lessons) scored higher in spatial task ability than those who had not. The March 1999 issue of ***Neurological Research*** describes a study led by Gordon Shaw (University of California, Irvine) which showed improved math scores among elementary school children who took piano lessons.

While the validity of the Rauscher and Shaw studies has been rigorously questioned by scholars and researchers, they have received press coverage that has raised interest in early childhood music among the general public.

Most importantly, the study of music at a young age increases the quality of the child's early life experiences. Music can soothe, stimulate or entertain children. It provides pleasure, joy and an outlet for creative expression; it helps develop listening and auditory discrimination skills; it contributes to motor skill development (both large muscle and small muscle); and it increases the range and flexibility of the voice. Music can soothe emotions, invite enthusiasm and bring immense pleasure to the listener.

Reasons for Music in the Early Childhood Classroom

The influences of music go far beyond the intellectual and physical development of a child. Music experiences contribute to the growth of well-balanced children in sensitivity, expressiveness, and the spirit essential for functioning in a complicated world. Learning about music in a classroom setting provides growth for children in other areas.

1. **Sharing:** Learning to share materials and to take turns in music activities, such as playing instruments, helps reinforce patience and respect for others in the group.
2. **Confidence and Poise:** Music making offers children a chance to perform with and for others, and to develop confidence in their ability to make presentations for groups.

[1]Howard Gardner, *Frames of Mind* (New York: Basic Books), 1983, 99.

3. **Perseverance and Commitment:** As children become more skilled in singing, moving and playing instruments, they can see and hear the results of their efforts.
4. **Friendships:** Music activities often require interaction with peers in the class, which helps develop positive relationships among children.
5. **Coordination:** The many movement activities associated with music experiences develop both small muscles and large muscles. The awareness of internal steady pulse, coordinated with external movements, helps children regulate their behavior.
6. **Self-respect and Satisfaction:** As musical skills develop, children feel a strong sense of satisfaction in their progress and develop a feeling of self-respect that transfers to other situations in life.
7. **Creativity and Self-expression:** Music experiences often invite individual creative responses and encourage children's imagination in other creative endeavors.
8. **Pride in Achievement:** Sharing music with peers and family reinforces the value of each child in the classroom, and children develop a sense of pride in their musical achievements.
9. **Concentration and Problem-solving:** Learning about music requires concentration and focus. When children are asked to analyze, compare and contrast sounds, they are actively engaged in problem-solving experiences.
10. **Fun and Relaxation:** Singing, moving, playing instruments and listening to music are all enjoyable experiences. Music making can provide hours of personal entertainment and relaxation throughout one's entire life.

Characteristics of Four-, Five-, and Six-Year-Olds

Some characteristics of four-, five-, and six-year olds that affect musical learning include:

1. Students have an excitement and enthusiasm for learning.
2. Physical coordination increases each year.
3. Attention span is limited and curiosity is high.
4. To a great extent, learning depends on imitation. Demonstration is very important in the lesson. "Hands-on" experiences are more important than verbal explanations.
5. Physical activity (moving and responding to music) is an important part of learning.
6. The need for praise is powerful.
7. Memory is quick, but things are soon forgotten too. Consequently, repetition is important to the learning process.
8. Reality is seen in relationship to self and the environment.
9. Taking turns is an accepted part of daily life.
10. Students have a great desire to please the teacher.
11. They do not sit and listen to long verbal explanations.
12. They are enthusiastic singers and enjoy moving to music and playing singing games.
13. They are more attentive learners if the senses of touch, sight and sound are used in instruction.
14. They function well in group situations.
15. They enjoy expressing non-musical ideas through music.
16. They enjoy live musical performances.

Four-, five-, and six-year olds can be very different from each other. Five- and six-year olds especially enjoy companions of their own age and frequently have "play dates." As students grow older, they can respond more competently to the pulse of music and follow movement directions more exactly for traditional dances. Vocabulary and small muscle control increase with age. By the time children are six years old, they can play games with rules; often pair up and have best friends; have a need to win and be the center of attention; and show a high level of activity.

Special Considerations in Teaching Music to Young Children

Teaching music to young children (ages 4–6) in a classroom setting can provide a natural way to involve children in developing expressive behaviors. The following principles will aid the classroom teacher in working with music in the early childhood classroom:

1. The materials used in lessons should involve many musical behaviors such as singing, movement and playing instruments. These experiences are not intended to focus on performance as the final goal, but rather to give young children a broad range of musical avenues for expression.

2. The materials used in lessons should take into consideration the level of visual representation that is meaningful to young children. Movement and playing instruments precede graphic and symbolic visuals, which lead to simple concepts using traditional musical notation.

3. Young children learn in a cyclic manner and need repeated encounters with materials to process experiences. Lessons should include many opportunities to review and repeat familiar musical activities.

4. Young children do not view music as isolated from other classroom activities, and will often create their own musical expressions in their play. Musical experiences in the classroom should encourage this type of independent music making.

The National Standards for Music Education

Music Educators National Conference (MENC) has published learning standards in the areas of music, dance, drama and visual art in *The National Standards for Arts Education: What Every Young American Should Know and Be Able to Do.*[1] The music standards for young children are described in two separate documents, one with a focus on pre-K children (Appendix G, p. 129), and the other focusing on K–4 learners (Appendix H, p. 130).

The lessons in *Classroom Music for Little Mozarts* were designed to address music learning standards for children ages four, five and six. This age group encompasses standards from both documents. The following shows how *Classroom Music for Little Mozarts* activities approach these standards.

Classroom Music for Little Mozarts lessons incorporate a variety of music for singing. Styles include energetic gathering songs, folk songs, songs with motions and actions, and quiet lullabies.

Book 1 of *Classroom Music for Little Mozarts* also includes playing simple percussion instruments —sticks and shakers. Suggestions for the Music Center include instrument exploration and discovery, as well as playing rhythm patterns learned in the group lesson on the instruments.

Children are invited to improvise accompaniments through movement to many of the large group singing experiences in *Classroom Music for Little Mozarts.* In the Music Center, children are encouraged to create their own musical ideas and to play instruments as they sing.

Children use rhythm patterns they have learned to construct longer compositions. In the Music Center, they can develop their own ideas for sound making and constructing music.

The Big Music Book activities introduce children to the idea of "pictures of sound." The iconic representations in the early lessons transform into rhythmic notation in a simple fashion. In keeping with the idea of patterns of sound, the notation is simple. All notation-oriented lessons are preceded by opportunities for singing, movement and playing instruments. These active experiences prepare children to develop an awareness and understanding of the concept before learning the symbol.

Specific activities focus on children's listening skills. Movement is used to demonstrate understanding, as they move to the steady beat or play rhythm patterns on instruments. As they learn musical vocabulary, children can use appropriate verbal labels to describe the music they hear and perform. Children learn to identify same and different sounds, and then how to describe the ways sounds are varied (high/low, fast/slow, loud/soft). This is part of the analysis process in music learning for young children.

[1] *National Standards for Arts Education: What Every Young American Should Know and Be Able to Do.* Reston, VA: Music Educators National Conference, 1994.

Within the group lessons and the Music Center activities, children develop skills in performing music through singing, movement and playing instruments. As teachers encourage children to participate in these experiences, they help children evaluate their own performance with ways it can be changed or improved. The final lesson, a sharing with friends and family, is a culminating experience where children prepare their best work to share with others.

Each lesson is set in the context of an early childhood classroom, where all subjects and curriculum topics are part of a child's everyday environment. There are many opportunities for teachers to link the musical ideas with other classroom learning, especially in the areas of social skills, language skills and number concepts.

History is incorporated through the characters in the story. Mozart Mouse, Beethoven Bear, and Clara Schumann-Cat are based on actual musicians—Wolfgang Amadeus Mozart, Ludwig van Beethoven, and Clara Schumann. Clara refers to her musical family and describes ways she learned music by being a part of this history. The costumes worn by Mozart Mouse (lace collar) and Beethoven Bear (tuxedo-type coat) reflect the time period in which the real composers lived. Many of the other characters who appear in later books are also based on important figures in music history. The listening lessons provide many opportunities to link with history and culture. Bringing "live" musicians to the classroom could also address this standard.

Music and the Early Childhood Teacher

While the *Classroom Music for Little Mozarts* program can be taught by music teachers, it was designed so that early childhood classroom teachers also can teach it. The teacher plays a very important role in the success of the *Classroom Music for Little Mozarts* lessons. The teacher's attitude towards musical experiences contributes to the children's perceptions of the experience. If the teacher projects a positive attitude toward music lesson time, the children will be engaged by the enthusiasm.

Young children do not view music as a separate "subject area," nor do they expect a different teacher to teach them about music. With guidance from the classroom teacher, they will be eager to participate in the *Classroom Music for Little Mozarts* group lessons and in the suggested follow-up music play activities.

Some early childhood teachers may be concerned about their lack of experience as singers, and as a result, hesitate to sing with the children. Singing is a natural form of expression for children, and the *Classroom Music for Little Mozarts* lessons invite singing in many ways. For teachers who are uncertain about their own singing as a model for children, the recorded compact disc (CD) in the program provides a good vocal example. Use the CD to lead the group activities with songs. As children repeatedly hear the recorded songs, they will learn the melody and eventually sing along with the recording.

In recording the CD, careful attention was paid to the tempo of the songs (how fast or slow to sing), and to the best key for singing (whether a song is high or low to sing) with young children. If a song seems high in pitch to you, it may be that you have been singing in a more adult register of your voice. Children's pitch level is naturally higher than adults, because their vocal cords are shorter and produce higher pitches than adult voices do.

If a song is pitched too low for children to sing, they can simply chant or speak the text, without pitch. The difference between singing a song and chanting a rhyme is that the song has text, rhythm and pitch while the rhyme has only text and rhythm.

Rhythmic speech, sometimes called chanting, is a very important part of children's musical learning though fingerplays, rhymes and similar activities. Rhythmic speech reinforces the rules of speech and timing of language, and helps children in a group learn to work together. Underlying rhythmic speech is a steady beat, the foundation for group music making. If teachers are uncertain about their own singing voices, examples can be incorporated using such rhythmic speech in the classroom, while using the CD model for the songs.

Skills and Concepts Included in *Classroom Music for Little Mozarts*

Music experiences in the *Classroom Music for Little Mozarts* program develop general musicianship skills in listening, singing, playing classroom instruments (rhythmic activities), and structured and expressive movement. Understanding of musical symbols is also addressed with simple visual representations that lead to traditional musical notation. Musical concepts and vocabulary are incorporated into each lesson.

Listening

Children listen to music naturally. Research shows that children respond early to differences in volume (loud/soft) and to differences in the type of instrument or voice. Responding to pitch and rhythm patterns follows, with response to harmony (multiple sounds) coming later. Children's preferences for musical styles are not yet fixed at ages four, five, and six; research shows that they are open to listening to a wide variety of recorded music.

Listening examples in the *Classroom Music for Little Mozarts* include classical music, traditional folk music, and music composed specifically for the lessons. While listening to recorded music, children are often invited to move in creative and structured ways, and to engage in other activities such as coloring pages with illustrations of the lesson.

Singing

Singing plays an important role in early childhood music learning. Children can sing accurately at an early age. Some research supports the fact that a child's range of tones increases progressively from ages two through five. The most common range for group singing of young children involves the pitches D to A, just above middle C on the piano. This small range naturally limits the number of tunes that can be sung completely by the children. The songs in *Classroom Music for Little Mozarts* use both limited and expanded range to develop singing skills. Children should sing the songs or parts of songs that are comfortable for them, and listen to music that is beyond the natural singing range.

Singing is best taught by listening and repetition. The teacher and the compact disc provide models for the child to imitate. When learning to sing a song, young children often listen to it several times before joining in with the teacher or the CD. Teachers should be comfortable with the words of the song, and should encourage children's participation through movement and dramatization.

Three different types of songs are used in *Classroom Music for Little Mozarts:* familiar folk songs for interest and motivation; songs with words and motions to reinforce rhythm, melody and other music concepts; and songs to introduce expressive elements while stimulating creativity and musical imagination.

Playing Instruments

Playing percussion instruments is exciting for children. The tone colors of the various instruments (wooden clicking sounds, metal ringing sounds, thick drumming sounds) heighten the awareness of musical qualities and patterns. Since a percussion instrument is an extension of the body, children need to experience movement activities to prepare them to play the instruments.

The lessons in Book 1 of *Classroom Music for Little Mozarts* incorporate playing two simple classroom percussion instruments—wooden sticks and shakers. To play these instruments accurately, preparatory experiences are included for the children to explore the sound potential and develop the physical control for producing and changing the sound. In presenting a lesson that involves playing sticks "on the beat" or in a pattern, children also need some "free play" time with the sound-making objects, to experiment with sound qualities and control in playing. Both physical control (coordinated two-hand movements) and visual control are required for playing most instruments.

Instruments can be used for a variety of purposes in the music class. Beyond the exploratory sound-play appropriate for young children, the typical four- to six-year-old child can play the instruments in these more structured or representational ways:

1. **To support or replace body percussion (claps, stamps, etc.):** This type of instrument play requires the children to first be able to accurately place the beat in the appropriate place using sounds such as clapping or stamping. The instrument then replaces the body sound while incorporating a variety of interesting timbres into the music making.

2. **To add "color" and sound effects to stories, rhymes, recordings:** Instruments are often used to add ethnic color or style to words or recordings. Children can help make choices about appropriate instruments to use in different examples.

3. **To illustrate patterns or formal changes in music:** Instruments help divide the sections of a recorded composition or the phrases in a song. These formal ideas about music help children construct the whole of the musical performance.

Recommended Percussion Instruments

The following recommendations can be used as guidelines for instruments that produce the various types of musical sounds that can be used in classroom music teaching. Recommendations for numbers of instruments to purchase are suggested related to the number of children in the classroom:

Large Group (12–20 children)
Medium Group (6–11 children)
Small Group (fewer than 6 children)

<u>Non-pitched Instruments</u>

1. Hand Drums—clear, deep sounds for focused pulse and patterns
   - Large or Medium Group: 4–6
   - Small Group: one for each child
2. Sticks and Wood Blocks—clear, pointed sound for quick rhythms and patterns; length should be no more than 12 inches; plain wooden dowel-types are preferable to slim, colored sticks.
   - One pair of sticks for every child
   - 1–2 wood blocks for the classroom
3. Shakers—colorful or thicker sounds without clear center
   - Large Group: 4–6
   - Medium or Small Group: one pair for each child
4. Jingle Bells—shiny, uncentered sounds for color
   - Large or Medium Group: 2–3
   - Small Group: one per child
5. Gong and Triangle—shimmery sounds that last a long time, for cues and accents
   - 1–2 for the classroom

<u>Pitched Instuments</u>

Each classroom should have two pitched instruments for "conversational" music play and for playing melodies and melodic patterns. Examples of such instruments include xylophones and glockenspiels.

Movement

Two types of movement (free movement and structured movement) are connected to music learning in the early childhood years. Children are natural movers. They often use their bodies in free, fluid ways to express their own ideas and feelings or to dramatize characters from a story or song. These movements are not synchronized to musical ideas such as the steady beat.

Children also can learn to control their bodies in more coordinated ways, which can lead to synchronizing with musical ideas such as steady beat and rhythm patterns. Singing games with structured responses (placing an action on a specific beat) are other examples of this.

Movement experiences serve several important purposes in classes for young children:

1. Movement develops large motor coordination by moving to the steady pulse (beat) of the music.
2. Movement re-energizes children for increased concentration on highly focused activities in the music class.
3. Movement develops concentration through memorizing structured dance steps to music.
4. Movement stimulates the imagination and creative thinking through dramatic play while listening to music and singing.
5. Movement can demonstrate a young child's understanding of musical concepts and vocabulary.
6. Movement is a form of visual representation, which precedes verbal labels and explanations.
7. Movement is a form of representation that reinforces musical concepts and vocabulary.

In *Classroom Music for Little Mozarts,* opportunities for movement are included in every lesson. Children creatively dramatize song texts and add prescribed movements to songs and chants. Movement becomes a form of visual representation, making the "unseen" qualities of the musical experience become visual. The movement experiences in *Classroom Music for Little Mozarts* fall loosely into three categories:

Songs with Words and Motions: Songs with words and motions invite children to follow the directions in the text. Instructions for moving are part of the words of the song.

- *Hello Song*
- *If You're Happy and You Know It*
- *Do Re Mi Tapping Song*
- *Goodbye Song*

Structured Movement: Classroom experiences with structured movement help children with coordination and a sense of accurate timing. The following songs offer specific "spaces" where the expected movement response should be included.

- *Do You Know?*
- *Twinkle, Twinkle, Little Star*
- *High and Low Song*
- *Johnny Works with One Hammer*
- *Mozart Mouse's Song*
- *Mexican Hat Dance*

Creative Movement: These songs and recorded examples encourage children to dramatize the text or story of the song. Children can use their imagination to play the roles of characters within the songs.

- *The Itsy Bitsy Spider*
- *Racing Car*
- *Giant's Lullaby*
- *The Old Gray Cat*

Visual Representation (music reading)

Developing skills in reading music begins with the recognition that things—including sounds—can be named and labeled. Most lessons in *Classroom Music for Little Mozarts* include a brief segment that focuses on age-appropriate visual representations, ranging from pictorial ideas to signs.

These begin with simple illustrations of characters with their names (Mozart Mouse and Beethoven Bear). The next lessons include iconic images for concepts, such as a racing car for fast and a turtle for slow. The introduction of pictures for patterns of sound follows, e.g., one hammer equals one beat in *Johnny Works with One Hammer.* In the final lessons of Book 1, short segments of traditional musical notation are presented.

The idea of visual representations builds on children's playful encounters with literacy-based materials. The visual representations presented in *Classroom Music for Little Mozarts* build on the initial experiences during the lessons, as children are engaged in movement, singing, listening and instrument play. These experiences are then represented in the Big Music Book pages, where children move from pictorial representations (the characters in action moving up and down stairs or driving fast in the racing car) to iconic representations (hammers to show the steady beats). Symbols flow into the traditional musical notation signs.

Two music signs are introduced in Book 1, the quarter note and the quarter rest. These are presented in patterns—four quarter notes; three quarter notes and a quarter rest. The children then learn to combine these two patterns to create a longer pattern. In this manner, children gain physical and cognitive control over the brief patterns and learn to put them into longer rhythmic "compositions." This construction-type task is related to the work of actual musical composers.

Concepts and Vocabulary

At a young age, children can learn to label musical sounds, instruments, and ideas with appropriate musical terms. Research shows that young children often recognize changes in music but don't have the terminology to describe them.

In *Classroom Music for Little Mozarts,* most lessons focus on one new musical idea while reviewing others. Interactive experiences in the lesson reinforce the qualities of the focus idea through singing, movement and playing instruments.

Classroom and Individual Opportunities for Music Learning

Early childhood professionals advocate a variety of classroom learning experiences for young children. Children, ages four through six, are able to learn in group settings, but they also need time for individual exploration and discovery in the classroom. The *Classroom Music for Little Mozarts* program was designed to facilitate music teaching and learning in both group and individual environments.

Each of the ten lessons is carefully outlined to focus on group music learning. Specific vocabulary and concepts are introduced and reviewed in each lesson. All of the lessons begin with a song that invites children to come to make music together *(Hello Song)*. The reading of the story in each lesson also draws the children to the music circle, as they hear about the musical adventures of Beethoven Bear and Mozart Mouse. Together the children sing, move, listen, and play musical instruments as part of the full group, and they learn as a group about visual representations of sound through the Big Music Book.

The *Classroom Music for Little Mozarts* program also includes ideas for setting up a Music Center in the early childhood classroom, to allow for the play that is so important to learning at this age. The musical play space ideas are developed from the group lesson material and follow each lesson. The suggested experiences will help children build on the lesson concept, the musical vocabulary, the adventure story ideas, or the Big Music Book representations. Some of the musical play space activities can be done by individual students; others can be done by small groups of children; while some will need teacher guidance.

The Classroom Lesson Format

Classroom Music for Little Mozarts is organized as a series of ten lessons in which children encounter Mozart Mouse and Beethoven Bear, who live in their early childhood classroom. The adventures of these two delightful characters introduce or reinforce the musical experiences in each lesson.

Each lesson has a theme and a focus on a musical idea or concept. These proceed from simple introductions of the characters in Lesson 1 to specific musical content and skills in the following lessons. In the final lesson, Mozart Mouse and Beethoven Bear join in a shared musical performance for their friends, and they invite all the students to do the same.

Although the lessons are designed to be presented in ten sequential sessions, it is possible to divide the lessons in other ways to facilitate usage in the early childhood classroom. For example, a teacher could read the story from the lesson separately, at another time during the day. A teacher could also use the coloring pages with quiet listening as a separate activity.

Each lesson plan has four parts:

1. Teaching Materials—A list of teaching materials to aid the teacher in preparing and organizing the lesson
2. Lesson Overview—A brief summary of what is included in the various parts of the lesson
3. Detailed Lesson Plan—A step-by-step plan that enumerates what the teacher does in each section and responses that can be expected from the children
4. Ideas for Connections in the Music Center—Suggestions divided into general developmental areas including related children's literature

The Music Center

The Classroom Music for Little Mozarts program includes ten group music lessons that are led by the teacher. These are important in helping children work and play together as a musical group. Early childhood teachers know, however, that young children also need opportunities for self-directed learning, involving individual and small group experiences to explore, to create, to discover, and to process information. These experiences also reinforce the developmental behaviors by showing individual initiative, making choices, and problem solving.

The authors recommend that each classroom have a designated space for this type of musical play. The Music Center can be available to children at a general "free play" time as well as other times when children are able to choose activities in the classroom.

Each lesson recommends examples of items to place in the center to facilitate play related to the lesson content. These include:

- Small characters of Mozart Mouse, Beethoven Bear and Clara Schumann Cat
- Dress-up items
- Recordings with listening equipment
- Song cards (pictures to illustrate the songs in the lessons)
- Concept cards (pictures to illustrate the concepts in the lessons)
- Classroom instruments
- Children's books on musical themes

The Music Center ideas are organized to address both developmental and musical goals.

1. **Social/Language/Imagination:** In the first category the focus is on developmental behavior and sociodramatic play, where children can pretend to be the characters in the story. They can dress up as Mozart Mouse, or they can use small figures of the characters from the story. In this way, children learn that "one thing can stand for another," and thus build representational understanding.

2. **Musical Ideas:** The second category of play ideas offers suggestions for individual or small group musical experiences, including singing, listening and playing instruments. This gives children a chance to try some of the skills and concepts from the group lesson in a more personal manner.

3. **Musical/Representational:** The third category of play ideas in each lesson relates to the musical symbols used in the lesson. The incorporation of these pictorial ideas is another valuable step in developing literacy skills. As children learn to match auditory clues with visual symbols, they are incorporating prereading experiences.

4. **Other-Manipulatives:** The final category of play ideas presents a variety of other experiences, including recommended children's literature to place in the center. Books with musical themes, including books that illustrate children's songs, support the presence of music in the classroom and create links between the general classroom curriculum and music.

As the ten lessons unfold over time, the materials from each lesson can be left in the Music Center to create a continuing rich musical environment for play. Alternatively, the materials can be changed weekly to focus specifically on the new lesson concept or theme. Because of the possibility of "lots of sound" coming from the center, the teacher must decide on the maximum number of children who can be working in the Music Center at the same time. The authors recommend that teachers start with no more than two or three children at a time in the Music Center.

The Detailed Lesson Plans

The detailed lesson plans are divided into sections—Introduction and Review, Story Connections, Visual Representations, Extension and Elaboration, and Closing. Within each section, activities are enumerated in a suggested order of presentation for the teacher. In some cases, a script (indicated by the word *say*) is given for the teacher to suggest an exact wording to introduce an activity. More experienced teachers should feel free to vary the script. The appropriate student response follows each item in the list of activities.

Introduction and Review: The *Hello Song* always begins each lesson. The activities that follow review concepts, materials and activities from previous lessons.

Story Connections: Every lesson contains a segment of a story about the characters. This listening activity allows children to enter the imaginary and playful world of Mozart Mouse and Beethoven Bear as they learn about music, too. Segments of the story build on the previous ones to form one long story. Because the story is recorded on the CD as well as printed in the lesson plans and on pages 79–86 of this book, a teacher can choose to read the story or use the recording. The Big Music Book contains a page for each story segment that should be open as children listen to the story.

Visual Representation: This section of the lesson reinforces the musical concepts from the lesson using a second page from the Big Music Book. It focuses on the musical ideas and vocabulary from the lesson. Singing, listening, movement and instrument activities support this area.

Extension and Elaboration: This section further reinforces ideas from the lesson through additional activities in a variety of categories.

Closing: Closing activities always include a coloring page to reinforce the theme of each lesson. The pictures are related but not identical to the pictures in the Big Music Book. Children can color these individual pages and compile them into a booklet at the end of the ten-week program. The recording also includes music for the quiet listening experiences that are linked to the coloring pages. The teacher can discuss this music with the children or simply let it serve as background music. The *Goodbye Song* closes each class.

Pacing the Classroom Lesson

The lessons in *Classroom Music for Little Mozarts* were designed for 30–45 minute time segments. The actual time you need for the lesson may vary from that target number for a variety of reasons. Some lesson activities are marked "optional," and may be eliminated if time is a concern. The following suggestions aid with organizing the classroom lesson time.

1. The *Hello Song* invites the children to come to the music class and can be used as a transitional song from other classroom activities. Teachers can begin the recording while children are finishing or cleaning up from another activity. It can be played several times to draw the children to the circle.

2. In reading or listening to the story, you may want to question the children about what they heard in the story, or invite their own ideas about what might happen next. The lesson outline does not always include this exchange of ideas. While children's comments about their personal connections to the story will lengthen the story time portion of the lesson, the interaction can be positive in many ways.

3. When introducing new songs, play the CD as many times as necessary for the children to hear the model and any instructions in the song. Even if the plan or outline does not call for this repetition, it may be appropriate for your group.

4. The lessons are designed with a quiet listening experience at the end to provide a calm closing to the class as children color. Instead of always coming at the close of the group music time, this entire activity of listening and coloring can be scheduled at a different point in the day when a calm and quiet mood is desired. The listening experience can also be used on a completely different day in the week; this opportunity for review can be an effective learning experience for the children.

Lesson 1

New Music Friends

Musical Concept Emphasis: High and Low

Teaching Materials

- ❑ *Classroom Music for Little Mozarts* CD
- ❑ CD player
- ❑ *Classroom Music for Little Mozarts* Big Music Book, pages 4–5:

- ❑ Mozart Mouse, Beethoven Bear plush animals
- ❑ Xylophone, mallet
- ❑ Coloring sheet: copies of page 95 for each student:

- ❑ Crayons for each student

Lesson 1 Overview

Part 1: Introduction
- *Hello Song* (1)

Part 2: Story Connections (Big Music Book, page 4)
- Chapter 1—New Music Friends (2)

Part 3: Visual Representation (Big Music Book, page 5)
- Mozart Mouse likes high sounds. Beethoven Bear likes low sounds.
- *High and Low Song* (3)
- Demonstrate high and low sounds on the xylophone.

Part 4: Extension and Elaboration
- *If You're Happy and You Know It* (4)
- *Do You Know?* (5) *optional*

Part 5: Closing
- Color page 95 while listening to *High and Low Song* (3).
- *Goodbye Song* (30)

Part 1: Introduction

Teacher	Children
1. Play *Hello Song* (💿1) to indicate the start of music class.	1. Stand.

💿1

Hello Song

Piano Arrangement pages 106–107

Moderato (♩ = ca. 138) *mf*

This is such a hap-py day! Our mu-sic friends have come to play with Mo-zart Mouse

8 *rit.* *f* *a tempo* *mf*
and Bee-tho-ven Bear. Friends will come from far and near to hear the mu - sic

15 *molto rit.* *a tempo*
we will make to - day. Hel - lo, hel-lo, it's mu-sic time to-day. We're glad you're here; it's

21 *f* *gradually slowing*
time to sing and play. We'll clap our hands, *(clap)* stamp our feet, *(stamp)* turn a-round, *(turn around)* touch the ground. *(bend down)*

26 *a tempo* *mf*
Hel - lo, hel-lo, it's mu-sic time to-day. We're glad you're here; it's time to sing and play.

Teacher	Children
2. Demonstrate the movements in the lyrics: wave hello, clap hands, stamp feet, turn around, touch the ground.	2. Imitate teacher's movements.
3. Say: "We have two music friends who are joining us for music class. Listen to the beginning of the *Hello Song* to learn their names." • Play *Hello Song,* do motions and encourage children to sing.	3. Listen for the names of the music friends in the first part of the song. Sing and do the motions during the refrain.

Part 2: Story Connections

Teacher	Children
1. Introduce music friends Mozart Mouse and Beethoven Bear by showing the plush animals to the children.	Sit, watch and listen.
2. Say: "Today we have a story about the two special music friends who were mentioned in the *Hello Song,* Mozart Mouse and Beethoven Bear. When you listen to the story, you'll find out where they live, and you'll learn something about the music they like." • Show Big Music Book, page 4. • Read aloud **Chapter 1: New Music Friends** (CD 2).	

CD 2

Chapter 1: New Music Friends

Once upon a time, there was a school where children just about your age went every day. In that school, there was a wonderful classroom filled with all sorts of things to help the children learn. There was a big white board to write on, colorful bulletin boards with artwork, shelves filled with books to read, crayons and markers for drawing, tables where the children did their work, a Play Center filled with lots of toys, and even a Music Center with many musical instruments. But of all the things the children had in their classroom, their favorites were a little stuffed bear and a little stuffed mouse. Their names were Beethoven Bear and Mozart Mouse.

All day long, Beethoven Bear and Mozart Mouse sat quietly in the classroom, allowing the children to play with them during free time. But at night, Beethoven Bear and Mozart Mouse did something quite different! When the children went home and the teacher had locked the door, the little bear and little mouse would quickly turn on the lights and hurry from the little house in the Play Center where they lived, to their favorite place in the classroom—the Music Center. They spent many hours happily playing with the instruments.

One evening while they were playing, they discovered that some of the instruments made high sounds, and some made low sounds. Beethoven Bear said to Mozart Mouse, "I love to play low sounds!"

Mozart Mouse replied, "I think high sounds are the best!"

"No!" Beethoven Bear said, "Low sounds are better. They are perfect for a bear like me."

"No!" Mozart Mouse would reply. "The high sounds are perfect for a mouse like me."

And so went the conversation that Beethoven Bear and Mozart Mouse had many times when they played in the Music Center. Sometimes they would take a peek in the Big Music Book that the teacher always used in class. "This must be a really special book," said Beethoven Bear. Mozart Mouse added, "The children learn so many wonderful things from this book."

Beethoven Bear and Mozart Mouse invite you to join them in their musical adventures. They are your new music friends, and together they will take you on a journey through the exciting world of music.

Part 3: Visual Representation

Teacher	Children
1. Show Big Music Book, page 5. • Ask: "Is Mozart Mouse high or low on the page?" *[High]* • Ask: "Is Beethoven Bear high or low on the page?" *[Low]*	1. Sit, answer questions.
2. Show the Mozart Mouse plush animal, and use your high voice to say, "Mozart Mouse likes high sounds." Simultaneously hold Mozart Mouse up high. Show the Beethoven Bear plush animal and use your low voice to say, "Beethoven Bear likes low sounds." Simultaneously hold Beethoven Bear down low.	2. Sit, watch, listen.
3. Say: "Let's use our high voices to say 'Mozart Mouse.'" (Use high voice for the words *Mozart Mouse.*) ♩ ♩ ♩ Mo-zart Mouse	3. Echo, saying "Mozart Mouse" in a high voice.
4. Say: "Let's use our low voices to say 'Beethoven Bear.'" (Use low voice for the words *Beethoven Bear.*) 𝅗𝅥 ♩ ♩ 𝅗𝅥 Bee - tho-ven Bear	4. Echo, saying "Beethoven Bear" in a low voice.
5. Ask children to show high/low with their hands by raising them when saying "Mozart Mouse" and lowering them when saying "Beethoven Bear."	5. Raise hands while saying "Mozart Mouse" in a high voice, and lower hands while saying "Beethoven Bear" in a low voice.
6. Encourage individual response. • Ask: "Who can say 'Mozart Mouse' by yourself?" "Who can say 'Beethoven Bear' by yourself?"	6. Take turns demonstrating high or low with voice and hand position while saying "Mozart Mouse" or "Beethoven Bear."
7. Say: "Mozart Mouse and Beethoven Bear can help us listen to music that is high and low. Let's find out how they can help us." • Play *High and Low Song* (CD 3). See piano arrangement (pages 108–109). • Stand tall for high sections, bend down low for low sections. *[First section is HIGH and second section is LOW.]*	7. Listen and stand tall for high sections, bend down low for low sections.
8. Show the xylophone to the class. *(To avoid left/right confusion that can occur with a xylophone; hold it in a vertical manner with the shorter bars at the top.)* • Demonstrate that the shorter bars at the top of the xylophone sound high; and that the longer ones at the bottom of the xylophone sound low.	8. Sit, listen.

Part 4: Extension and Elaboration

Teacher	Children
1. Say: "You are very good high and low listeners! Listening to music makes Mozart Mouse and Beethoven Bear happy. They would like you to make some music for them, and show them you can be happy, too. How can you show them you're happy?"	1. Stand and offer suggestions on how to show they're 'happy.'
2. Ask students to show a big smile and do some other happy movements such as clapping hands, stamping feet, and jumping up high.	2. Respond to teacher's movement prompts.
3. Sing *If You're Happy and You Know It* (CD 4), demonstrating the motions. Invite the students to join you.	3. Imitate the motions of the teacher and begin to sing along.

4. Say: "That was great! Let's sing this song again for Mozart Mouse and Beethoven Bear."	4. Sing song and do the motions suggested by the lyrics.

Teacher	Children
Optional:	
5. Say: "Do you think Mozart Mouse and Beethoven Bear like our singing? Do you remember which one of them likes high sounds and which one likes low sounds?"	5. Respond to questions.
6. Say: "Let's listen to *Do You Know?* (5) and we'll answer the questions together. Then, we'll sing the song." • Sing *Do You Know?*	6. Listen, answer questions and sing.

Part 5: Closing

Teacher	Children
1. Pass out crayons and copies of coloring sheet, **New Music Friends,** page 95. • Play *High and Low Song,* (3), while children color.	1. Color **New Music Friends** coloring sheet.
2. Say: "Our music time is over for today. Now it's time for us to say good-bye to our music friends, Mozart Mouse and Beethoven Bear. They have a goodbye song to sing for us. Let's listen!" • Play *Goodbye Song,* (30), and act out the movements specified in the lyrics: take a bow, take a rest, wave goodbye.	2. Listen and imitate teacher's movements to the song.

Ideas for Connections in the Music Center

1. **Social/Language/Imagination**

   a. A picture of Mozart Mouse and Beethoven Bear on the sign for the Music Center.

   b. Invite pretend play (sociodramatic play) with Mozart Mouse and Beethoven Bear, such as acting out the story or making up a new story about the characters.

   c. Students can dress up as Mozart Mouse (ruffle collar) or Beethoven Bear (bow tie).

2. **Musical Ideas**

   a. Place pitched instruments such as a xylophone in the Music Center, to explore high and low sounds while encouraging self-discovery.

   b. Place cards with a picture of Mozart Mouse with the word *high,* and Beethoven Bear with the word *low,* in the Music Center.

3. **Musical/Representational**

   a. Make a Mozart Mouse card that includes a picture and the following sentence: I like ________ sounds. Children can find a word card that reads *high* to match it, and say or play high sounds. Make a similar card with Beethoven Bear and low sounds.

   b. Find pictures of things that represent high and low sounds, such as a bird for high sounds and a tugboat for low sounds. Students match the pictures to the words *high* and *low.*

4. **Other—Manipulatives**

   a. Place stickers of Mozart Mouse and Beethoven Bear on the appropriate xylophone bars. (A *Music for Little Mozarts Sticker Book* [20647] is available from music dealers.)

   b. Put pictures of Mozart Mouse and Beethoven Bear on magnets for students to place on a magnetic board to illustrate high and low.

Lesson 2

Moving to Music

Musical Concept Emphasis: Up and Down

Teaching Materials

- ❑ *Classroom Music for Little Mozarts* CD
- ❑ CD player
- ❑ *Classroom Music for Little Mozarts* Big Music Book, pages 6–7:

- ❑ Mozart Mouse, Beethoven Bear plush animals
- ❑ Xylophone, mallet
- ❑ Coloring sheet: copies of page 96 for each student:

- ❑ Crayons for each student

Lesson 2 Overview

Part 1: Introduction
- *Hello Song* (1)
- Review high and low with xylophone.
- *High and Low Song* (3)
  Play 'Follow the Leader' game.

Part 2: Story Connections (Big Music Book, page 6)
- **Chapter 2—Moving to Music (6)**

Part 3: Visual Representation (Big Music Book, page 7)
- *The Itsy Bitsy Spider* (7)

Part 4: Extension and Elaboration
- Play up and down patterns on xylophone.
- Introduce glissando with voice.
- *If You're Happy and You Know It* (4)
  a) Sing, with motions.
  b) *(Optional)* Sing high/low verses to the melody of *If You're Happy and You Know It*.

Part 5: Closing
- Color page 96 while listening to *The Itsy Bitsy Spider* (7).
- *Goodbye Song* (30)

Part 1: Introduction and Review

Teacher	Children
1. Play *Hello Song* (1) to indicate the start of music class. (See page 17 for lyrics.) • Demonstrate the movements in the lyrics: wave hello, clap hands, stamp feet, turn around, touch the ground.	1. Stand, sing and imitate teacher's movements.
2. Ask: "What were the names of the music friends we met at our last class? They liked high and low sounds." *[Mozart Mouse and Beethoven Bear]*	2. Raise hands, answer question.
3. Using xylophone, demonstrate high and low sounds.	3. Sit, watch and listen.
4. After several examples, say: "Let's show Mozart Mouse and Beethoven Bear that we know high and low sounds. If the sounds are high, put your hands straight up in the air and whisper *Mozart Mouse.* If the sounds are low, put your hands in your lap and whisper *Beethoven Bear.*" • Play more examples on the xylophone. Match student movement for each example, by holding Mozart Mouse or Beethoven Bear in the correct position (high or low) to reinforce children's responses.	4. Listen to musical examples and respond appropriately.
5. Show the Beethoven Bear and Mozart Mouse plush animals. • Say: "Beethoven Bear and Mozart Mouse are going to help us play Follow the Leader as we listen to the *High and Low Song.* Let's make a line." • Give the Mozart Mouse plush animal to the leader at the front of the line to hold, and the Beethoven Bear plush animal to the leader at the end of the line.	5. Stand, form a line.
6. Say: "Now we're going to play Follow the Leader. When you hear the high parts of the song, follow Mozart Mouse. When you hear the low parts, turn and follow Beethoven Bear." *[First section is HIGH and second section is LOW.]* • Play *High and Low Song* (3)	6. Stand, follow the leader, listen for high and low.

Part 2: Story Connections

Teacher	Children
Say: "Our music friends, Mozart Mouse and Beethoven Bear are going to have some more adventures in the Music Center. Let's find out what they're doing today." • Show Big Music Book, page 6. • Read aloud **Chapter 2: Moving to Music** (CD 6).	Sit, watch and listen.

CD 6

Chapter 2: Moving to Music

One evening, Beethoven Bear and Mozart Mouse were playing in the Music Center as usual. Beethoven Bear was playing low sounds, and Mozart Mouse was playing high sounds. As they were playing, they noticed something different about the xylophone. "Look!" Mozart Mouse said to his friend. "The xylophone is leaning against the wood block, and it looks almost like stairs. I'm going to climb it." And with that, Mozart Mouse began to climb the xylophone.

"Hey!" Beethoven Bear exclaimed. "Did you hear what happened to the sound?" He was certain that he had just made an important discovery. "It started low and got higher as you climbed up. I want to try that, too."

Beethoven Bear scurried up the instrument to join his friend at the top. "I've never seen the classroom from up here before," Beethoven Bear remarked. They stood quietly, admiring the view. Then suddenly, they heard a noise!

"What is that?" Beethoven Bear whispered to Mozart Mouse. "Quick!" Mozart Mouse advised his friend. "Slide down the xylophone and hide."

The sound that came from sliding down the xylophone made them giggle. "That was fun!" Beethoven Bear squealed with delight. "Shh," Mozart Mouse warned. "I think someone is coming in."

The two friends huddled together behind the instruments, wondering what would happen next.

Part 3: Visual Representation

Teacher	Children
1. Show picture in the Big Music Book (page 7) of Beethoven Bear walking down the stairs and Mozart Mouse walking up the stairs to illustrate the direction of the sound. • Say: "Up, up, up, up" to follow Mozart Mouse up the stairs; and "Down, down, down, down" to follow Beethoven Bear down the stairs.	1. Say: (with teacher) "Up, up, up, up" to follow Mozart Mouse up the stairs; and "Down, down, down, down" to follow Beethoven Bear down the stairs.
2. Say: "*The Itsy Bitsy Spider* can help us learn about up and down. The spider will go up the waterspout, then down. Let's sing the song with the motions." • Play *The Itsy Bitsy Spider* (7), do motions and encourage the children to sing.	2. Sit, sing with motions.

Part 4: Extension and Elaboration

Teacher	Children
1. Say: "We can pretend that Beethoven Bear and Mozart Mouse are stepping up and stepping down the stairs on our xylophone." • Play up and down patterns on the xylophone. • Say: "Now we have *musical stairs.*"	1. Sit, watch, listen.
2. Say: "Sometimes it's fun to step up and then slide down—just like climbing up the steps of a slide at the playground, then sliding down. Can you slide *up* with your body? That would be hard to do! But your *voice* can slide UP. . . And your voice can slide DOWN." • Teacher demonstrates vocal glissando. (A 'glissando' is a group of notes that slide from a low pitch to a high pitch, or slide from a high pitch to a low pitch.) • Say: "Let's sing notes in the direction my hand moves."	2. Perform a vocal glissando following the movements of the teacher's hand from low to high or high to low.
3. Sing *If You're Happy and You Know It* with CD 4. (See page 20 for lyrics.)	3. Sing *If You're Happy and You Know It.*
4. ***(Optional)*** Say: "Good job! Now let's clap our hands first high and then low when we sing *If You're Happy and You Know It.*" • Sing without CD: "If you're happy and you know it, clap up high! *(clap hands high in the air)* If you're happy and you know it, clap down low! *(clap hands low, near the floor)* If you're happy and you know it, Then your smile will surely show it, If you're happy and you know it, clap high/low." *(clap once high and once low.)*	4. Stand, copy the teacher's movements.

Part 5: Closing

Teacher	Children
1. Pass out crayons and copies of coloring sheet, **Moving to Music,** page 96. • Play *The Itsy Bitsy Spider,* (CD 7), while children color.	1. Color **Moving to Music** coloring sheet.
2. Say: "Now it's time for us to sing good-bye to our music friends, Mozart Mouse and Beethoven Bear." • Sing *Goodbye Song,* (CD 30). (See page 22 for lyrics.)	2. Sing and do movements.

Ideas for Connections in the Music Center

1. **Social/Language/Imagination**

   a. Place images of a seesaw and a slide in the Music Center to represent up and down in students' everyday lives.

   b. Children can use the Mozart Mouse and Beethoven Bear plush animals to represent going up and down. They can add vocal sounds (glissandos) to match the up and down movements of the characters.

   c. Act out *The Itsy Bitsy Spider* by pretending to be the spider, the rain and the sun.

2. **Musical Ideas**

   a. Encourage play with the xylophone (playing each pitch separately) to move up and down.

   b. Connect the vocal sound registers (low, high) with movements—slide between low and high sounds.

   c. Discover movements to represent up and down sounds.

3. **Musical/Representational**

   a. Encourage the students to use arrows to indicate direction of the musical sounds.

   b. Use markers on a whiteboard to draw a "picture" of the sounds moving from high to low and low to high.

4. **Other—Manipulatives**

   a. Identify other things that can have up and down characteristics, such as an airplane, a bird, a fire engine siren, a slinky, a kite, the sun rising and setting during the course of a day. Many things can represent up *or* down, but it is more difficult to find things that move *between* the two extremes.

   b. Find pictures or things in the classroom that move *between* up and down.

   c. Read books that explore up and down, such as:

      The Berenstain Bears Inside, Outside, Upside Down, by Stan and Jan Berenstain, Random House, 1997.

      What's Up, What's Down? by Lola M. Schaefer, Greenwillow, 2002.

Lesson 3

Sound and More Sound

Musical Concept Emphasis: Loud and Soft

Teaching Materials

- ❑ *Classroom Music for Little Mozarts* CD
- ❑ CD player
- ❑ *Classroom Music for Little Mozarts* Big Music Book, pages 8–9:

- ❑ Mozart Mouse, Beethoven Bear plush animals
- ❑ Xylophone, mallet
- ❑ Coloring sheet: copies of page 97 for each student:

- ❑ Crayons for each student

Lesson 3 Overview

Part 1: Introduction
- *Hello Song* (1)
- Up and Down:
  - a) Review with Big Music Book picture, page 7.
  - b) Follow pitches of xylophone with hands or bodies.
  - c) Glissando.
- *Racing Car* (8)

Part 2: Story Connections (Big Music Book, page 8)
- **Chapter 3—Sound and More Sound (9)**

Part 3: Visual Representation (Big Music Book, page 9)
- Categorize pictures.

Part 4: Extension and Elaboration
- *The Itsy Bitsy Spider* (7)
- *Giant's Lullaby* (10)

Part 5: Closing
- Color page 97 while listening to Beethoven's *Rage Over the Lost Penny* (11).
- *Goodbye Song* (30)

Part 1: Introduction and Review

Teacher	Children
1. Sing *Hello Song* (1) with movements. (See page 17 for lyrics.)	1. Stand. Sing and imitate teacher's movements.
2. Show picture in Big Music Book (page 7) of Beethoven Bear and Mozart Mouse walking up and down the stairs. • Ask: "Who is walking up and who is walking down?" *[Mozart Mouse walks up; Beethoven Bear walks down.]*	2. Answer question.
3. Play xylophone examples of pitches that move up or down. • Say: "Is this sound going up or down? Use your hands to follow the direction of the sounds." • Invite individual children to play the xylophone, moving up or down. The class identifies the direction. • Or, you say the direction, the child plays, and class evaluates for accuracy.	3. Identify the direction of the sounds. Use hands to follow the direction of the sounds.
4. Say: "You remembered up and down very well. Let's see if you remember the 'glissando.' Who can show me how a glissando looks with your hands, and sounds with your voice?" *[Sliding up and down.]*	4. Show "glissando" with their hands and voices.
5. Say: "Mozart Mouse and Beethoven Bear know a song about a racing car. It has a glissando in it. We're going to listen for the glissando and show it with our hands. Climb into your racing car, and listen for the 'zoom'. Put your hands on the wheel and let's go!" • Make side-to-side movements with pretend steering wheel as if turning the wheel. When you get to the word "zoom," use a "lift-off" movement, raising hands up.	5. Stand, copy the teacher's movements.
6. Perform *Racing Car* with 8.	6. Perform *Racing Car*.

Part 2: Story Connections

Teacher	Children
Say: "The words "ready, set, zoom" helped us get our racing cars moving. Now let's get "ready, set, and listen" to find out what's happening to Mozart Mouse and Beethoven Bear today. As our last story ended, Beethoven Bear and Mozart Mouse were hiding behind some instruments because they heard someone coming into the classroom. Let's find out who it is!" • Show Big Music Book, page 8. • Read aloud **Chapter 3: Sound and More Sound** (CD 9).	Sit and listen.

CD 9

Chapter 3: Sound and More Sound

The key turned in the lock, and someone opened the door to the classroom. Mozart Mouse peeked out from behind the big drum where he and Beethoven Bear were hiding. He let out a sigh of relief.

"It's only the teacher, Ms. Tina," he whispered to Beethoven Bear. He and Beethoven Bear went to the Music Center every day to listen as she taught music to the children.

Ms. Tina walked over to the Music Center. She opened up the Big Music Book. As she looked at the book, she began to play a few of the instruments one at a time. Some of the instruments made soft sounds and some of them made loud sounds. Mozart Mouse liked to hear her play.

"I think she's planning tomorrow's music lesson," Mozart Mouse reported to his friend. Soon, Ms. Tina finished. She closed the book and walked to the door. After turning off the lights, she closed the door behind her and locked it. Beethoven Bear and Mozart Mouse had learned to listen for the sound of the key in the lock. It meant that they were free to play for the rest of the evening without any interruptions.

The first thing Beethoven Bear did was find the drums. He began to play as loudly as he could.

"Hey! You'd better be quiet!" Mozart Mouse cautioned his friend. "Ms. Tina might hear us."

"Oops," said Beethoven Bear, "I was having so much fun, I forgot!"

"Why don't you play something with a soft sound like this?" Mozart Mouse suggested, as he picked up the triangle and struck it lightly. He handed the triangle to Beethoven Bear, who began to play it quietly.

Mozart Mouse had other plans that evening. Earlier in the day, he had heard the children singing a song about a racing car. He couldn't wait to drive the little red toy car that the children loved to race around the room. Soon, Mozart Mouse was zooming in and out between the tables and chairs in the classroom.

"I feel just like a race car driver!" he thought to himself.

He looked at the clock on the classroom wall and came to a screeching halt beside Beethoven Bear. "Time for bed, my friend," he said. "Hop in, and I'll give you a ride home."

Mozart Mouse parked the car next to the little house. The two friends got out and climbed the stairs to the second floor where their cozy beds were waiting for them. As they snuggled under the covers, Mozart Mouse began to hum a quiet lullaby to his friend.

"Goodnight," Mozart Mouse whispered to Beethoven Bear when he was finished. But Beethoven Bear was already fast asleep, dreaming about the adventures that they would have the next day.

Part 3: Visual Representation

Teacher	Children
Say: "In the story, Mozart Mouse and Beethoven Bear are playing loud and soft sounds. Let's look at some pictures in the Big Music Book (page 9) and decide which of these make loud sounds and which make soft sounds."	Sit, categorize pictures as loud or soft.

Part 4: Extension and Elaboration

Teacher	Children
1. Say: "Sometimes music is loud, and sometimes music is soft. We can sing *The Itsy, Bitsy Spider* soft or loud. First, we'll sit and sing it softly with small movements. Then we'll stand and sing about the 'Great Big Spider' loudly with large movements." • Say: "Show me your small spider movements. Good! Now show me your BIG spider movements. Excellent, let's sing." • Play *The Itsy Bitsy Spider* (CD **7**). (See page 27 for lyrics.)	1. Sing with motions.
2. Say: "That was LOUD singing! What's a good place to sing a loud song? *[playground, ball game]* What's a good place to sing a soft song? *[inside the house, to a baby]*	2. Answer questions.
3. Say: "A song that helps a baby go to sleep is called a 'lullaby.'" • Ask: "Why do we sing lullabies softly?" *[To help babies sleep]*	3. Answer questions.
4. Listen quietly to *Giant's Lullaby* (CD **10**), while pretending to rock a baby or a sleeping Mozart Mouse.	4. Sit, pretend to rock a baby.

Part 5: Closing

Teacher	Children
1. Pass out crayons and copies of coloring sheet, **Sound and More Sound,** page 97. • Play Beethoven's *Rage Over the Lost Penny* (CD **11**), while children color.	1. Color **Sound and More Sound** coloring sheet.
2. Say: "Before you all zoom off in your racing cars, Mozart Mouse and Beethoven Bear would like to sing the *Goodbye Song.* Let's join them using our soft voices." • Sing *Goodbye Song* (CD **30**). (See page 22 for lyrics.)	2. Sing and do movements.

Ideas for Connections in the Music Center

1. Social/Language/Imagination

Use a baby doll and blanket to encourage quiet talk and singing lullabies.

2. Musical Ideas

a. Explore differences in sounds between two instruments, such as a big drum for loud sounds and a triangle for soft sounds.

b. Use movement to respond to recorded music that is loud or soft. Scarves can encourage movement.

c. Change the playing from loud to soft on the same instrument.

d. Use an inexpensive microphone to demonstrate loud and soft voices.

3. Musical/Representational

Make a stop-sign visual, with the word *loud* on one side and *soft* on the other. Children can play "traffic cop," changing the instruction for a friend who is playing instruments in the Music Center.

4. Other—Matching and Classifying

a. Find pictures of animals or environmental items that make loud and soft sounds. Have students sort them into two groups.

b. Read books that explore loud and soft, such as:

Mortimer, by Michael Martchenk, Firefly Books, 1985.

Thump, Thump, Rat-a-Tat-Tat, by Gene Baer, Harper Collins Juvenile Books, 1991.

Lesson 4

Speed Limits

Musical Concept Emphasis: Fast and Slow

Teaching Materials

- ❑ *Classroom Music for Little Mozarts* CD
- ❑ CD player
- ❑ *Classroom Music for Little Mozarts* Big Music Book, pages 10–11:
- ❑ Mozart Mouse, Beethoven Bear and Clara Schumann-Cat plush animals
- ❑ Crayons for each student
- ❑ Coloring sheet: copies of page 98 for each student:

Fast and Slow

Lesson 4 Overview

Part 1: Introduction
- *Hello Song* (1)

Part 2: Story Connections (Big Music Book, page 10)
- Chapter 4—Speed Limits (13)

Part 3: Visual Representation (Big Music Book, page 11)
- Discuss Mozart Mouse and Beethoven Bear picture with the road signs.

Part 4: Extension and Elaboration
- *Racing Car* (8)
- *Giant's Lullaby* (10)
- *The Old Gray Cat* (14) Sing, play game

Part 5: Closing
- Color page 98 while listening to Haydn's *Surprise Symphony* (12).
- *Goodbye Song* (30)

Part 1: Introduction and Review

Teacher	Children
Sing Hello Song (1) with movements. (See page 17 for lyrics.)	Stand. Sing and imitate teacher's movements.

Part 2: Story Connections

Teacher	Children
Say: "Let's see what Beethoven Bear and Mozart Mouse are doing this week. Last time, we read about Mozart Mouse and Beethoven Bear's discovery of loud and soft sounds when Ms. Tina came back into the classroom to plan the next music lesson. Today's story begins the very next morning." • Show Big Music Book, page 10. • Read aloud **Chapter 4: Speed Limits** (13).	Sit and listen.

13

Chapter 4: Speed Limits

The next morning, Mozart Mouse lay in bed with his eyes closed. He thought he heard singing. It was a song about a cat. For a moment, he forgot where he was. Then he sat up and sneezed, "Ah-choo!"

"Oh, dear," he thought to himself. "I hope there isn't a cat in the room. I am very allergic to cats." Then, he looked at the clock on the nightstand. It was already 9:00 a.m. He and Beethoven Bear had overslept! The singing he heard was coming from the Music Center. The children had already started their music lesson for the day!

He jumped out of bed and went over to wake up Beethoven Bear.

"We've got to hurry," he urged his friend. "We might miss something important."

They ran quickly down the stairs and climbed into the toy racing car. Mozart Mouse drove as fast as he could to the other side of the room. It wasn't easy, because the children had scattered toys all over the floor. It looked like an obstacle course as he drove in and out.

"Slow down!" Beethoven Bear urged. "You are driving too fast!"

Suddenly, something large loomed ahead of them. From out of nowhere, a big, white, furry ball appeared. Mozart Mouse stepped on the brakes. Beethoven Bear covered his eyes. It looked as if they were going to run into a giant cotton ball!

The little red racing car went slower and slower until it finally came to a stop. Beethoven Bear opened his eyes. What he thought was a giant cotton ball was, in fact, a beautiful white cat.

Part 3: Visual Representation

Teacher	Children
Show Big Music Book, page 11. Discuss pictures of Mozart Mouse and Beethoven Bear. Show students the road signs in the picture. • Ask: "Is Mozart Mouse going fast or slow?" *[Fast]* • Ask: "Is Beethoven Bear going fast or slow?" *[Slow]* • How can you tell?" *[Mozart Mouse is in a race car. Beethoven Bear is riding a turtle.]*	Sit, answer questions.

Part 4: Extension and Elaboration

Teacher	Children
1. Say: "Music can be fast or slow just as we can walk fast or slow, or run fast or slow." • Model moving in place: fast (run) then slow (jog).	1. Move in place, imitating teacher's movements.
2. Say: "Now let's climb into our racing cars and say, 'Ready, set, zoom.'" Add a honking horn motion on "beep-beep-beep." • Sing and do motions to *Racing Car* (8).	2. Do motions and say, "Ready, set, zoom," while acting out the song.
3. Say: "Our racing cars were small and fast. What if we were driving a GREAT BIG TRUCK? Or a GIANT EARTHMOVER? Then we would move very slowly. What if you were a great, big GIANT? Let's move around the room [or in place] to the music, taking giant steps." • Play *Giant's Lullaby* (10).	3. Move to the music slowly, as a giant would.
4. Say: "You did such a nice job moving to that slow song. The next song we're going to hear has some fast and slow parts. *The Old Gray Cat* tells a story about a sleeping cat and some playful mice." • Play *The Old Gray Cat* (14), listen to lyrics.	4. Sit and listen.

5. Choose some children to be mice, and some to be cats.
    - Play *The Old Gray Cat* (14).
    - Act out the story and sing the song.
    - At the end of the song, all the little mice are "safe" when they scamper back to their places.

5. Sing and act out the song.

Part 5: Closing

Teacher	Children
1. Pass out crayons and copies of coloring sheet, **Speed Limits,** page 98. • Play Haydn's *Surprise Symphony* (CD **12**) while children color.	1. Color **Speed Limits** coloring sheet.
2. Say: "Before you all zoom off in your racing cars, Mozart Mouse and Beethoven Bear would like to sing goodbye." • Sing the *Goodbye Song* (CD **30**). (See page 22 for lyrics.)	2. Sing and do movements.

Ideas for Connections in the Music Center

1. Social/Language/Imagination

Place small racing cars in the Music Center for pretend play.

2. Musical Ideas

Place shakers in the Music Center to explore fast and slow playing.

3. Musical/Representational

a. In the Music Center, place a picture of Mozart Mouse and Beethoven Bear in their racing cars, with the word *fast* written on it.

b. In the Music Center, place a picture of Mozart Mouse and Beethoven Bear riding a turtle, with the word *slow* written on it.

c. Make a stop sign with *fast* and *slow* on opposite sides. Have students take turns being the "traffic cop" as other students drive racing cars.

4. Other—Matching and Classifying

a. Identify animals, people and forms of transportation that move fast and slow.

b. Make speed limit signs and place them around the classroom in appropriate places.

c. Read books that explore fast and slow, such as:

Go, Dog, Go! by Philip D. Eastman, Random House, 1961

Start Your Engines, by Mark Todd, Callaway Editions, 2000

My Race Car, by Michael Rex, Henry Holt & Company, Inc., 2000

Lesson 5
Try This!

Musical Concept Emphasis: Skills and Vocabulary

Teaching Materials

- ❑ *Classroom Music for Little Mozarts* CD
- ❑ CD player
- ❑ *Classroom Music for Little Mozarts* Big Music Book, pages 12–13:

- ❑ Mozart Mouse, Beethoven Bear and Clara Schumann-Cat plush animals
- ❑ Xylophone, mallet
- ❑ Shakers, 1 for each student
- ❑ Coloring sheet: copies of page 99 for each student:

- ❑ Crayons for each student

Lesson 5 Overview

Part 1: Introduction
- *Hello Song* (1)

Part 2: Story Connections (Big Music Book, page 12)
- **Chapter 5—Try This! (15)**

Part 3: Visual Representation (Big Music Book, page 13)
- Discuss contrasting pictures.

Part 4: Extension and Elaboration
- Review high and low with xylophone.
- *High and Low Song* (3)
  Play Follow the Leader game.
- *The Old Gray Cat* (14)
  a) Review loud/soft, fast/slow verses.
  b) Sing, play game.
- Shake shakers—slow, fast, high, low.
- *Twinkle, Twinkle, Little Star* (16)

Part 5: Closing
- Color page 99 while listening to Mozart's *Variations on Twinkle, Twinkle, Little Star* (17).
- *Goodbye Song* (30)

Part 1: Introduction and Review

Teacher	Children
Sing *Hello Song* (CD 1) with movements. (See page 17 for lyrics.)	Stand. Sing and imitate teacher's motions.

Part 2: Story Connections

Teacher	Children
Say: "Our story ended last week when the little red toy racing car led our two music friends right to a beautiful white cat. I can't wait to see what happens next!" • Show Big Music Book, page 12. • Read aloud **Chapter 5: Try This!** (CD 15).	Sit, watch and listen.

CD 15

Chapter 5: Try This!

Beethoven Bear and Mozart Mouse sat in the car, too terrified to speak. They had almost run into the beautiful white cat!

"I beg your pardon," the cat purred. "You seem to be in quite a hurry. Is there a problem?"

Mozart Mouse cleared his throat nervously and spoke. "Please excuse us! We are late for music time," he looked around the room and continued, "but there were quite a few toys in our way."

"Allow me to help you," the cat offered. "Climb on my back, and I will take you to the Music Center."

Mozart Mouse wasn't at all sure what to do. If he got anywhere near the cat, he was certain he would start sneezing. On the other hand, if he didn't let the cat help them, he and Beethoven Bear would probably miss the music lesson.

"Thank you," he said hesitantly. Then, he got out of the car and climbed up to take a seat on top of the furry cat. Beethoven Bear followed him. They held on tightly as the cat walked slowly toward the children seated in the Music Center.

When they arrived, the two friends slid down to the floor and scrambled to get a good view of what the children were doing. Ms. Tina was teaching the class a song about an old gray cat. They were singing loud and soft and fast and slow. The Big Music Book was open to a picture of Mozart Mouse and Beethoven Bear going up and down the stairs of the playhouse. *[Show page 7 of Big Music Book.]*

"That's us in the picture!" Beethoven Bear said proudly to the cat.

"Oh, I already know who you are," the cat purred. "You're Beethoven Bear and Mozart Mouse. The children talk about you all the time."

"That's odd," Mozart Mouse thought to himself. "How would this cat know the children?"

He cleared his throat. "If you please, won't you tell us your name?" he asked shyly.

"It would be my pleasure," was the reply, "as soon as the teacher finishes reviewing high and low sounds."

Mozart Mouse was amazed! Who was this cat, and how did she know things about music? And why wasn't he sneezing?

Part 3: Visual Representation

Teacher	Children
Say: "The cat in the classroom knows a lot about music! Let's find out how much *you've* learned." Show Big Music Book, page 13. Discuss contrasting pictures (high/low, up/down, loud/soft, fast/slow). For each picture, say: "What is Mozart Mouse is doing? What is Beethoven Bear doing?" *[They are doing opposite actions from each other.]*	Sit, answer questions.

Part 4: Extension and Elaboration

Teacher	Children
1. Using xylophone, demonstrate high and low sounds.	1. Sit, watch and listen.
2. After several examples, say: "Let's show Mozart Mouse and Beethoven Bear that we know about high and low. If you hear a low sound, make a statue low to the ground. Everyone show me your "low" statue. Good job! If you hear a high sound, make a statue that stands up tall. Everyone show me your "high" statue. Good, let's begin." • Play more examples on the xylophone. Match student movement for each example by moving Mozart Mouse and Beethoven Bear plush animals to correct position in the air (high or low) to reinforce children's responses.	2. Stand, listen to musical examples and respond appropriately.
3. Show children Beethoven Bear and Mozart Mouse plush animals. • Say: "Beethoven Bear and Mozart Mouse are going to help us listen to the *High and Low Song.* Let's make a line." • Give Mozart Mouse to the leader at the front of the line to hold, and Beethoven Bear to the leader at the end of the line to hold.	3. Stand, form a line.
4. Say: "Let's play Follow the Leader. When you hear the high part of the song, follow Mozart Mouse. When you hear the low part, turn and follow Beethoven Bear. *[First section is HIGH; second section is LOW.]* • Play *High and Low Song* (3)	4. Stand, follow the leader, listen for low and high.
5. Say: "Let's sing *The Old Gray Cat* (14), and use our hands, just like this, to show how loud or soft we're singing." Teacher demonstrates that soft is a little space between the hands; loud is a wide space between the hands. Teacher models during the singing of the song.	5. Sing *The Old Gray Cat.*
6. Say: "Show me with your hands how big the sound is for each question. Soft would be only a little space between your hands. Loud would be a big space between your hands." • "When the cat was sleeping, was the music soft or loud?" *[Soft]* • "When the mice were scampering, was the music soft or loud?" *[Loud]*	6. Listen, answer questions using hands.
7. Choose some children to be mice, and some to be cats. • Play *The Old Gray Cat* (14). (See pages 38–39 for lyrics.) • Act out the story and sing the song. • At the end of the song, all the little mice are "safe" when they scamper back to their places.	7. Sing and act out the song.
8. Place a basket of shakers in the center of the circle. • Say: "That was some great scampering in *The Old Gray Cat!* When I point to you, show me how the mice were quietly creeping as you go to the basket for a shaker. Then show me how the cat was creeping as you return to your place."	8. Quietly go to basket for a shaker; then return to their place in the circle.
9. Say: "Shake the shakers slow, as if the mice were creeping."	

Teacher	Children
"Shake the shakers fast, as if the mice were scampering." "Shake the shakers high." "Shake the shakers low."	9. Stand, follow teacher's directions.
10. Say: "Let's sing a song we all know, *Twinkle, Twinkle Little Star,* using the shakers." • Play *Twinkle, Twinkle, Little Star* (16). Sing and model shaking shakers to the rhythm of the words.	10. Sing, imitate teacher playing shakers.

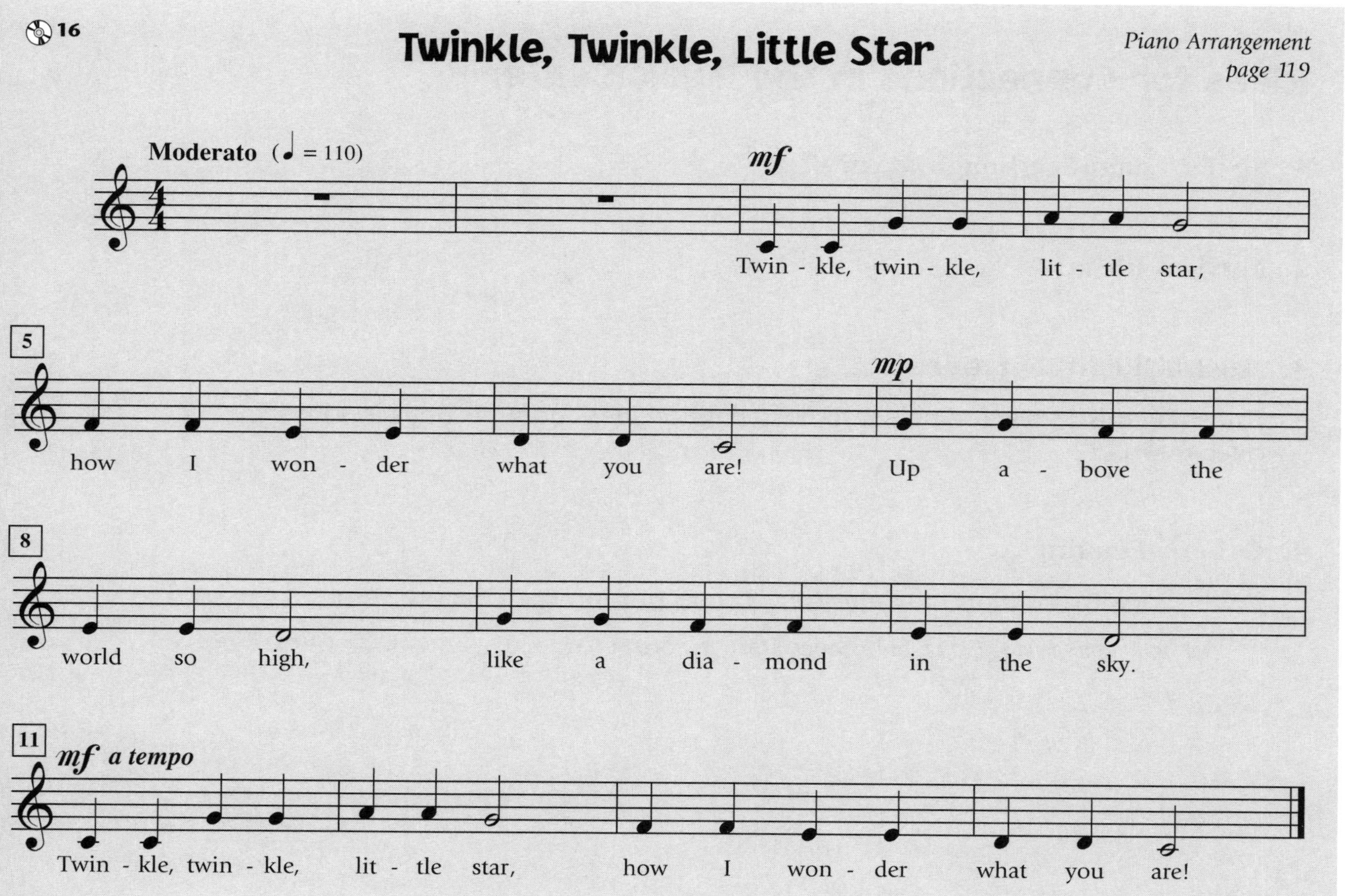

Teacher	Children
11. *(Optional)* Say: "Now we're going to sing *Twinkle, Twinkle, Little Star* in a new way. We are going to sing it without the recording so we can change the speed ourselves. Let's shake our shakers slowly as we sing *Twinkle, Twinkle, Little Star.*" • Teacher leads singing. • Say: "Now let's sing *Twinkle, Twinkle, Little Star* a little faster while we shake our shakers.	11. Listen and sing, playing shakers at appropriate speeds to match the singing.

Part 5: Closing

Teacher	Children
1. Pass out crayons and copies of coloring sheet, **Try This!** page 99. • Play Mozart's *Variations on Twinkle, Twinkle, Little Star* (CD **17**) while children color.	1. Color **Try This!** coloring sheet.
2. Say: "Now it's time to say goodbye to our music friends, Mozart Mouse and Beethoven Bear." • Sing the *Goodbye Song* (CD **30**). (See page 22 for lyrics.)	2. Sing and do movements.

Ideas for Connections in the Music Center

1. Social/Language/Imagination

2. Musical Ideas

3. Musical/Representational

Following this review lesson, continue to develop ideas from previous lessons in categories 1–3.

4. Other—Reading

Read a book that explores the musical concepts previously studied, such as:

A High, Low, Near, Far, Loud, Quiet Story, by Nina Crews, Greenwillow, 1999.

Lesson 6

Get That Beat!

Musical Concept Emphasis: Steady Beat

Teaching Materials

- ❑ *Classroom Music for Little Mozarts* CD
- ❑ CD player
- ❑ *Classroom Music for Little Mozarts* Big Music Book, pages 14–15:

- ❑ Mozart Mouse, Beethoven Bear and Clara Schumann-Cat plush animals
- ❑ Rhythm sticks, 1 pair for each student
- ❑ Crayons for each student
- ❑ Coloring sheet: copies of page 100 for each student:

Lesson 6 Overview

Part 1: Introduction
- *Hello Song* (1)
- *The Old Gray Cat* (14)
  Sing and move.

Part 2: Story Connections (Big Music Book, page 14)
- **Chapter 6—Get That Beat! (18)**

Part 3: Visual Representation (Big Music Book, page 15)
- *Do, Re, Mi Tapping Song* (19)
  Sing and move.

Part 4: Extension and Elaboration
- *Johnny Works with One Hammer* (20)
  a) Add hammer motions, keep steady beat.
  b) Explain rules for using sticks.
  c) Add sticks to song.

Part 5: Closing
- Color page 100 while listening to Sousa's *Stars and Stripes Forever* (21).
- *Goodbye Song* (30)

Part 1: Introduction and Review

Teacher	Children
1. Sing *Hello Song* (1) with movements. (See page 17 for lyrics.)	1. Stand. Sing and imitate teacher's motions.
2. Sing *The Old Gray Cat* (14) without movements. (See pages 38–39 for lyrics.)	2. Sing *The Old Gray Cat* without movements.
3. Choose some children to be mice, and some to be cats. • Act out the story and sing the song.	3. Sing and act out *The Old Gray Cat.*

Part 2: Story Connections

Teacher	Children
Say: "It's time for us to hear what our friends, Beethoven Bear and Mozart Mouse are doing today. The cat that carried Mozart Mouse and Beethoven Bear to the Music Center seems to know a lot about music. Mozart Mouse is wondering why this is so. Let's see if we can find out more about her, too." • Show Big Music Book, page 14. • Read aloud **Chapter 6: Get That Beat!** (18).	Sit, watch and listen.

18

Chapter 6: Get That Beat!

Mozart Mouse, Beethoven Bear, and the beautiful white cat watched and listened to the music lesson. When the teacher finished the lesson, the cat turned to them and smiled. "My name is Clara Schumann-Cat," she began. She purred happily as she told Beethoven Bear and Mozart Mouse about her musical background. "Everyone in my family plays the piano," she said proudly. "In fact, my great-grandmother was taught by Clara Schumann herself. Clara Schumann played the piano and composed music. She was very famous, you know. My mother named me after her."

"It's an honor to meet you," Beethoven Bear and Mozart Mouse said. Then Mozart Mouse continued, "We're forgetting our manners. Thank you so much for bringing us to the Music Center. We never would have made it without you. But if you don't mind my asking, what are you doing here in our classroom?"

"Don't you know?" Clara asked with surprise. The two friends shook their heads.

"Why, I am Ms. Tina's cat," she explained. "Sometimes she brings me to school, and I sit quietly and watch everything that happens in class. I'm surprised we never met before."

Just then, a steady hammering sound, *tap, tap, tap, tap,* interrupted their conversation.

"What's that?" Beethoven Bear asked.

"Someone must be doing some hammering in the next room," Clara replied. "The steady beat reminds me of a song. Do you know this?" She started to sing *Johnny Works with One Hammer.*

Mozart Mouse and Beethoven Bear quickly joined in, admiring how Clara had taken the sound of the hammer and quickly turned it into a music lesson. She gave each of them a pair of sticks, and they tapped a steady beat as they sang.

"That was fun!" Beethoven Bear exclaimed. "Can we do it again?"

"I can think of something even better," Mozart Mouse said. He turned to Clara and asked, "You seem to know so much about music. Could you give us music lessons?"

Clara Schumann-Cat was beaming. "I've always wanted to teach!" she exclaimed. "Teaching runs in my family, of course. Why don't we meet in the Music Center every day? We can start tomorrow."

"I can't wait!" Beethoven Bear said as he waved goodbye to Clara. He and Mozart Mouse walked back to their car and got in to drive home. "Tomorrow is going to be a special day," he said to Mozart Mouse.

"This time, I'm going to set my alarm clock," Mozart Mouse said. "We don't want to be late."

Part 3: Visual Representation

Teacher	Children
1. Show Big Music Book, page 15. Say: "These pictures are showing us something in music. What are these pictures showing us?" *[Different ways to keep a steady beat.]*	1. Answer question.
2. Say: "We will have to listen to directions for where to tap the beat in our next song, the *Do, Re, Mi Tapping Song.*" • Play the *Do, Re, Mi Tapping Song* (CD **19**). • Sing with recording, model the movements.	2. Stand and imitate teacher's movements; gradually add singing.

19

Do, Re, Mi Tapping Song

Piano Arrangement
pages 120–121

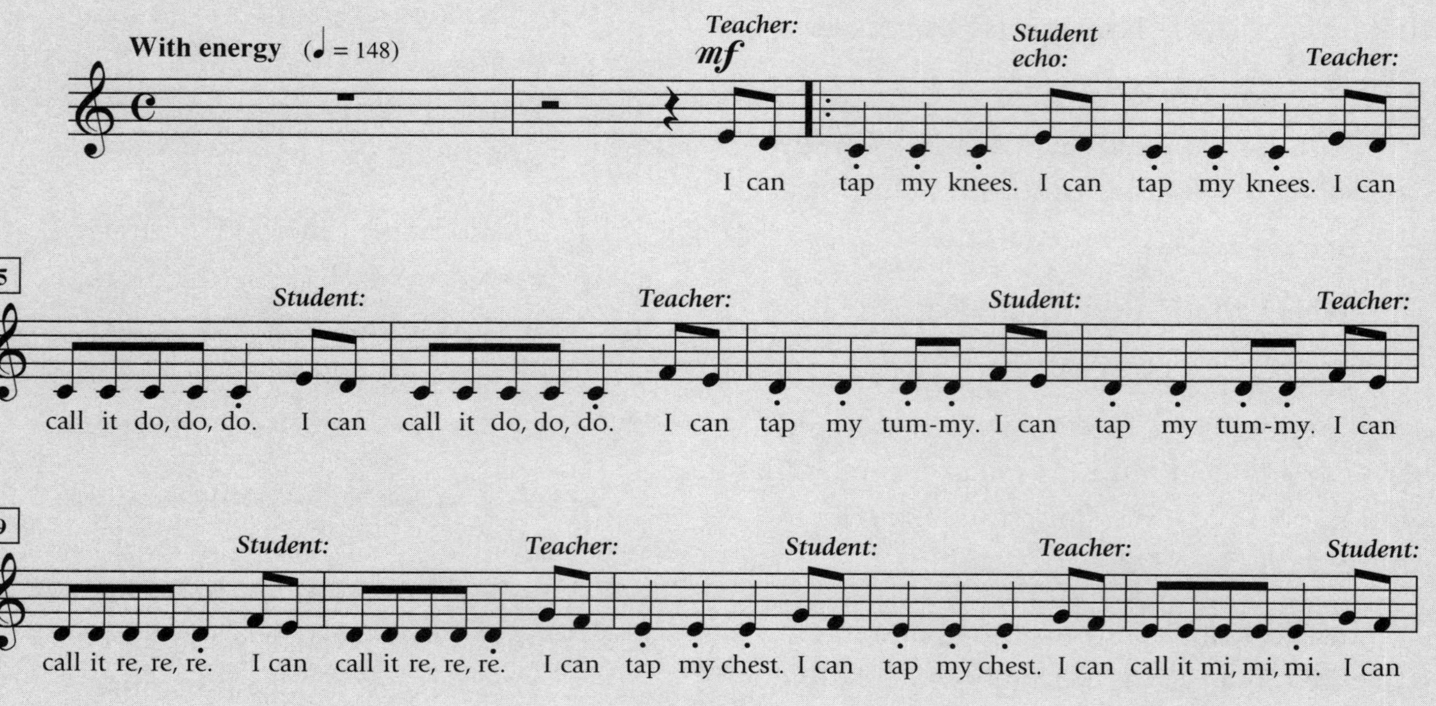

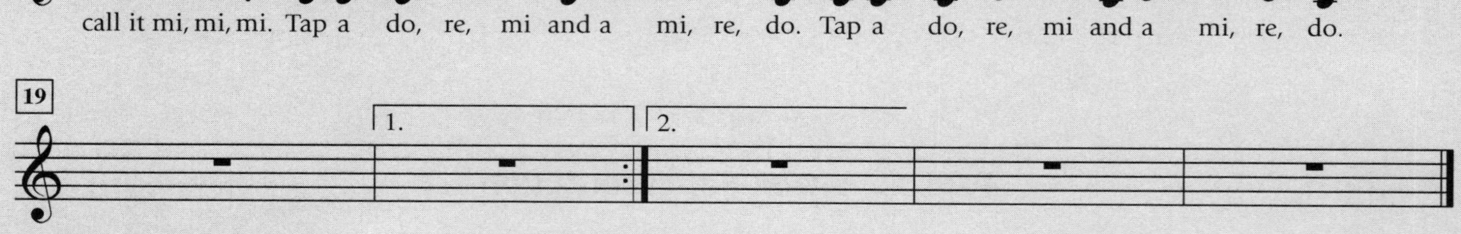

Part 4: Extension and Elaboration

Teacher	Children
1. Say: "You were great listeners and followed the directions very well. Sometimes we can do steady tapping motions even when the music has different words." • Play *Johnny Works With One Hammer* (20). • Add hammer motions, keeping the steady beat. • Invite children to sing along when they are ready.	1. Stand and imitate teacher's motions, keeping the steady beat. Gradually add singing.

20

Johnny Works with One Hammer

Piano Arrangement
pages 121–123

Part 4: Extension and Elaboration (continued)

Teacher	Children
2. Say: "You showed such steady hammering with your hands, your feet, and your head! Let's add one more thing to our hammering song. Today we'll use sticks. You can see that there are a lot of sticks in the box. When we play them for music class, we each need two sticks." (Show two sticks, one in each hand.) • "How many sticks do I have?" *[Two]* • "Yes! And where are my sticks?" *[One in each hand]*	2. Listen and answer questions.
3. Say: "We have some special things to remember when we're playing instruments. First, we have to be safe. For sticks, we need to have enough 'elbow room' so that we don't hurt anyone." • Demonstrate for students: put the ends of two sticks together and extend your elbows to illustrate how much room is needed. Say: "What can you do if you need more room?" *[Move.]*	3. Sit, listen and answer questions.
4. Say: "Everyone needs two sticks, one for each hand. When I call your name, please come to the instrument box. Take two sticks and then go back to your place."	4. Listen to directions, get sticks.
5. Say: "Let's try playing our sticks." • Demonstrate one (or both) of the following playing techniques: a) Hold one stick stationary to form a target, and hit it with the second stick. b) Use the sticks as a hammer and nail (acting out the text of the song, you would tap the end of one stick with the other).	5. Sit, watch, try playing sticks.
6. Sing *Johnny Works with One Hammer* (CD **20**) using the rhythm sticks to keep the steady beat.	6. Sing *Johnny Works with One Hammer* using the rhythm sticks to keep the steady beat.
7. Say: "Good job! When I call your name, please put your sticks in the box and go to your seat."	7. Sit, follow directions.

Part 5: Closing

Teacher	Children
1. Pass out crayons and copies of coloring sheet, **Get That Beat!** page 100. • Play Sousa's *Stars and Stripes Forever* (CD **21**) while children color.	1. Color **Get That Beat!** coloring sheet.
2. Say: "Now it's time to say goodbye to our music friends, Mozart Mouse and Beethoven Bear." • Sing the *Goodbye Song* (CD **30**). (See page 22 for lyrics.)	2. Sing and do movements.

Ideas for Connections in the Music Center

1. Social/Language/Imagination

a. Put plastic tools or picture of tools in the Music Center to use with *Johnny Works with One Hammer.* Encourage the students to change the lyrics to fit the instruments. Example: Julie works with one wrench, etc.

b. Dramatize a marching band, with props including band hats and a baton.

2. Musical Ideas

a. Place pairs of sticks in the Music Center and encourage the children to use them with *Johnny Works With One Hammer.*

b. Play a recording of *Stars and Stripes Forever* and pretend to have a marching band.

3. Musical/Representational

Make picture cards with one hammer, two hammers, three hammers, four hammers and five hammers to use with *Johnny Works With One Hammer.*

4. Other—Reading

Read books that explore steady beat, such as:

Chicka Chicka Boom Boom, by John Archambault, Aladdin Library, 2000.

The House That Jack Built, by Diana Mayo, Child's Play International, Ltd., 1995.

Lesson 7
Music Signs

Musical Concept Emphasis: Quarter Notes

Teaching Materials

- ❑ *Classroom Music for Little Mozarts* CD
- ❑ CD player
- ❑ *Classroom Music for Little Mozarts* Big Music Book, pages 16–17:

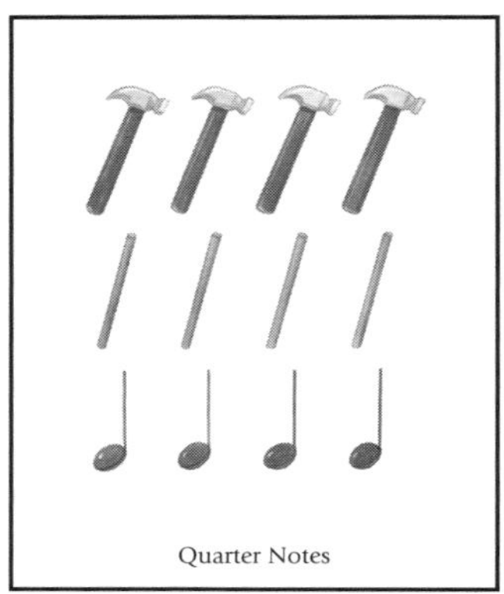

- ❑ Mozart Mouse, Beethoven Bear and Clara Schumann-Cat plush animals
- ❑ Rhythm sticks, 1 pair for each student
- ❑ Crayons for each student
- ❑ Coloring sheet: copies of page 101 for each student:

Lesson 7 Overview

Part 1: Introduction
- *Hello Song* (1)
- *Do, Re, Mi Tapping Song* (19)

Part 2: Story Connections (Big Music Book, page 16)
- **Chapter 7—Music Signs (22)**

Part 3: Visual Representation (Big Music Book, page 17)
- Look at hammer and stick notation.
- Play sticks, echoing teacher.

Part 4: Extension and Elaboration
- Match rhythms of words to visual notation.
- *Racing Car* (8) Sing with movements.

Part 5: Closing
- Color page 101 while listening to Bach's *Musette in D* (23).
- *Goodbye Song* (30)

Part 1: Introduction and Review

Teacher	Children
1. Sing *Hello Song* (CD 1) with movements. (See page 17 for lyrics.) 2. Say, "Let's sing the *Do, Re, Mi Tapping Song.*" (CD 19). (See page 50 for lyrics.) • Sing with recording, do the movements.	1. Stand, sing and imitate teacher's movements. 2. Stand, sing and imitate teacher's movements.

Part 2: Story Connections

Teacher	Children
Say: "I wonder what our music friends Beethoven Bear and Mozart Mouse are doing this week. In our last story, we found out the cat's name. Who remembers what her name was? *[Clara Schumann-Cat]* She is going to give Beethoven Bear and Mozart Mouse music lessons, and today is their first one." • Show Big Music Book, page 16. • Read aloud **Chapter 7—Music Signs** (CD 22).	Sit, watch and listen.

22

Chapter 7: Music Signs

Mozart Mouse's alarm clock rang very early the next morning. He and Beethoven Bear dressed quickly, ate breakfast, and drove to the Music Center in the toy car. The clock in the room said that it was only 7:00 a.m. Even the children weren't there yet!

Beethoven Bear picked up a pair of sticks and started tapping. "Doesn't this sound like the steady beat we made yesterday?" he asked. Mozart Mouse got a pair of sticks and joined in. They sang the song that Clara Schumann-Cat had taught them.

When they had finished, they heard a steady beat at the door, *tap, tap, tap, tap.* Mozart Mouse ran to see who it could be. He opened the door just a little so that he could peek out. It was Clara Schumann-Cat. "Hi, Clara. You're early," he greeted her.

"I know," she purred as she walked into the room, "but I just couldn't wait to teach my first music lesson. I could hear your sticks when I was at the door. You have a wonderful steady beat." She walked over to the Big Music Book and opened it. "Please join me over here. I would like to show you something," she said as she turned to the page that she wanted. "Now that you know what a steady beat *feels* and *sounds* like, we can see what a steady beat *looks* like." She pointed to the page and showed them how to tap the pattern. "This pattern is made up of four quarter notes," Clara explained. "Let's play this quarter note pattern again."

Beethoven Bear couldn't believe how easy and fun quarter notes could be. "I could do this all day!" he exclaimed as he ran around the Music Center playing quarter note patterns on all of the instruments.

Clara Schumann-Cat looked at the clock. "Shhh! I think it's time for the children to get here," she said in a whisper. She invited them to join her on the big pillow where they could sit and watch what the children did during music time that day.

To their surprise, the teacher turned to the same page that Clara had showed them in the Big Music Book. Mozart Mouse and Beethoven Bear were thrilled. They spent the rest of the day with Clara on her pillow, quietly singing and tapping quarter note patterns.

Part 3: Visual Representation

Teacher	Children
1. Say: "Last time we used sticks to help keep the steady beat of the hammers in *Johnny Works With One Hammer.* We can show the steady beat of hammers and sticks by making a picture of the sounds we made." • Show hammer and stick notation in Big Music Book, page 17:	1. Sit, watch and listen.
2. Say: "When I call your name, please take a pair of sticks from the box and return to your place."	2. Sit, follow directions.
3. Say: "Let's play our sticks using these stick pictures": • Demonstrate playing 4 even taps. Say: "Now you try it with me." • Prepare children by saying in rhythm: "1–2–ready–play." • Teacher should point to the stick notation (from left to right) as children play.	3. Sit, play sticks.
4. Say: "Let's put our sticks down in front of us. There is one more special part that we can add to our stick pictures on the page to make them look like "real" music. Every stick picture needs a little egg-shape [or oval if that term is familiar to children] near the bottom." • Show Big Music Book, page 17.	4. Watch, listen.
5. Say: "These music signs are called quarter notes. Every time we see one, we play one time on our sticks. Let's pick up our sticks and play quarter notes together." • Teacher should point to the quarter notes (from left to right) as children play.	5. Sit, listen, play.
6. Say: "When I say your name, please come to the center and put your sticks in the box."	6. Listen, return sticks to the box.

Part 4: Extension and Elaboration

Teacher	Children
1. Say: "Let's play a matching game to find some words that match our quarter note pattern." (♩ ♩ ♩ ♩) • Determine whether the following words or phrases are a match to the quarter note pattern in the Big Music Book. • Say: "Is this a match?" Clap the rhythm of the words and say: a.) "su-per scoot-er" *[4 beats—Yes]* b.) "old gray cat" *[3 beats—No]* c.) "rac-ing car" *[3 beats—No]* d.) "danc-ing mous-ie" *[4 beats—Yes]* e.) "hel-i-cop-ter" *[4 beats—Yes]*	1. Sit, listen, answer questions.
2. Say: "We've been sitting for a long time. Let's all 'rev up' our racing cars and go for a ride!" • Sing and do motions for *Racing Car* (CD **8**).	2. Stand, sing and imitate teacher's motions.
3. Say: "What wonderful race car drivers you are! I think that Mozart Mouse and Beethoven Bear must be smiling at your great 'zoom' movements. Now, let's change gears and go to our places for some coloring."	3. Listen, go to coloring places.

Part 5: Closing

Teacher	Children
1. Pass out crayons and copies of **Music Signs** coloring sheet, page 101. • Play Bach's *Musette in D* (CD **23**) while children color.	1. Color **Music Signs** coloring sheet.
2. Say: "Now it's time for us to sing goodbye to our music friends, Mozart Mouse and Beethoven Bear." • Sing the *Goodbye Song* (CD **30**). (See page 22 for lyrics.)	2. Sing and do movements.

Ideas for Connections in the Music Center

1. Social/Language/Imagination

a. Pictures of signs that children see regularly in daily life—such as those for fast food chains, grocery stores, chain stores, stop signs and speed limit signs—should be included in the Music Center.

b. Children can make signs to help them recognize things that they see regularly.

2. Musical Ideas

Show students staff paper with music written on it (both hand-written and engraved) so they see how signs represent sound.

3. Musical/Representational

A whiteboard or magnetic board can be used with circular magnets representing quarter notes. Students can practice putting the magnets on the board to form the pattern of four quarter notes. A *Music for Little Mozarts* magnetic Music Activity Board (19747) is available from music dealers.

4. Other

a. Ask students to draw pictures of signs that they know and color them.

b. Read books that explore signs, such as:

I Read Signs, by Tana Hoban, HarperTrophy, 1987.

Red, Yellow, Green: What Do Signs Mean? by Joan Holub, Cartwheel Books, 1998.

Lesson 8

Quiet, Please!

Musical Concept Emphasis: Quarter Rest

Teaching Materials

- ❑ *Classroom Music for Little Mozarts* CD
- ❑ CD player
- ❑ *Classroom Music for Little Mozarts* Big Music Book, pages 18–19:

Quarter Rest

- ❑ Mozart Mouse, Beethoven Bear and Clara Schumann-Cat plush animals
- ❑ Rhythm sticks, 1 pair for each student
- ❑ Crayons for each student
- ❑ Coloring sheet: copies of page 102 for each student:

Lesson 8 Overview

Part 1: Introduction
- *Hello Song* (1)
- *Do, Re, Mi Tapping Song* (19)
  Sing with movements.

Part 2: Story Connections (Big Music Book, page 18)
- **Chapter 8—Quiet, Please! (24)**

Part 3: Visual Representation (Big Music Book, page 19)
- *Mozart Mouse's Song* (25)
  Sing and add movement pattern.
  a) Introduce quarter rest pattern: ♩ ♩ ♩ 𝄽
  b) Tap pattern and say, "Mo-zart Mouse."

Part 4: Extension and Elaboration
- Tap patterns with sticks, echo teacher.
- *Mexican Hat Dance* (26)
  Walk in a circle, freeze at quarter rest.

Part 5: Closing
- Color page 102 while listening to Beethoven's *Symphony No. 5 in C Minor* (27).
- *Goodbye Song* (30)

Part 1: Introduction and Review

Teacher	Children
1. Sing *Hello Song* (💿**1**) with movements. (See page 17 for lyrics.)	1. Stand, sing and imitate teacher's motions.
2. Sing *Do, Re, Mi Tapping Song* (💿**19**)	2. Stand, sing and imitate teacher's motions.

Part 2: Story Connections

Teacher	Children
Say: "In our story last week, Clara Schumann-Cat taught our music friends all about quarter notes at their first music lesson. Let's listen and find out what Beethoven Bear and Mozart Mouse are learning today." • Show Big Music Book, page 18. • Read aloud **Chapter 8—Quiet, Please!** (💿**24**).	Sit, watch and listen.

Chapter 8: Quiet, Please!

Mozart Mouse and Beethoven Bear decided that they should get up early every day and go to the Music Center before the children got to school. One morning they were looking in the Big Music Book at a page with a quarter note pattern. But there was another pattern on the page that they had never seen before.

"What do you suppose this is?" asked Beethoven Bear, pointing to a squiggly line after three quarter notes.

"I don't know," Mozart Mouse answered, "but Clara Schumann-Cat will. She knows *everything.*" He sighed. "Do you think we'll ever know as much as she does?" he asked.

"I sure hope so," Beethoven Bear replied. "I'd like to be a music teacher some day." Then he thought for a moment. "I know one question she might not be able to answer."

"What?" Mozart Mouse asked.

Beethoven Bear giggled and said, "Why don't you ever sneeze when she is around? I thought you were really allergic to cats!"

Mozart Mouse giggled, too. "I am!" he exclaimed. "But I guess I'm not allergic to *musical* cats," he said.

"I hope you're right," Beethoven Bear said earnestly. "I wish Clara would get here soon so that we could find out what this is," he added, looking at the book again.

Just then, they heard a *tap, tap, tap, tap* on the door. "I'll bet that's Clara!" said Mozart Mouse as he ran to open the door. Clara walked into the room, ready to begin her lesson. She called them over to the Big Music Book.

"Oh," she began, "I see that you are on the very page I wanted to talk about today." She showed them the pattern from the song *Johnny Works with One Hammer.* They tapped it together. Then she pointed to the other pattern that had Beethoven Bear and Mozart Mouse puzzled, and said, "The squiggly line means silence. It is a quarter rest."

"*Now* I know what that is!" Beethoven Bear said as he pointed to the end of the pattern.

"Excellent!" said Clara. "Let's read and tap this pattern."

When they had finished, Mozart Mouse had made an exciting discovery. "That is just like the pattern in my name," he announced. "Listen," he said, and he began to chant his name and whisper *shh* after it: "Mo-zart-Mouse, *shh;* Mo-zart-Mouse, *shh.*"

Beethoven Bear was giggling again. "The pattern for your name has a symbol for silence in it—a quarter rest. That must be why mice are so quiet!"

Everyone laughed. Clara Schumann-Cat was pleased. "You both learned our lesson very well today. The patterns you learned have a special music name—they are called rhythm patterns. Would you like to play the new rhythm pattern on some instruments before the children get here?" she asked.

Mozart Mouse and Beethoven Bear ran happily to the instruments. Of course Beethoven Bear chose the big drum because he liked low sounds so much. Mozart Mouse chose the triangle so that he could hear his favorite high sounds. Clara's tail swished back and forth to the beat as the music friends played their new rhythm pattern over and over again.

Part 3: Visual Representation

Teacher	Children
1. Say: "Let's listen to a song about our music friend, Mozart Mouse. It includes the rhythm patterns that Clara Schumann-Cat taught Mozart Mouse and Beethoven Bear." • Play *Mozart Mouse's Song* (25) and sing.	1. Sit, listen.

Teacher	Children
2. Say: "Now, let's learn the tapping movements for the song." • Sing *Mozart Mouse's Song* (25), tap this pattern: ♩ ♩ ♩ 𝄽 a) Begin by putting out one palm flat. b) Use it as the 'instrument' and use the other hand as the 'mallet' to tap the rhythm of the text. c) Beats 1, 2, 3—tap the pulse lightly into the palm of one hand. d) Beat 4—close the 'mallet' hand into a fist, pull away.	2. Imitate teacher's movements.
3. Say: "Now, look at this rhythm in the Big Music Book." (page 19) (♩ ♩ ♩ 𝄽) It is different from the quarter note pattern (♩ ♩ ♩ ♩) we learned in our last lesson. What do you see that's different?" *[𝄽]* • Say: "One of these symbols means silence. *[𝄽]* It is called a quarter rest. Is it at the beginning or the end of the pattern?" *[end]*	3. Sit, watch, answer questions.
4. Say: "Let's tap this rhythm." • Tap and point to rhythm. Repeat several times. • Let's tap again. This time, say "Moz-art Mouse, rest" evenly while tapping the rhythm. (Repeat)	4. Sit, say and tap rhythm.
5. Say: "Now, let's sing *Mozart Mouse's Song,* and tap the rhythm." (25) • Point to rhythm as children sing song.	5. Sing, tap, read rhythm.

Part 4: Extension and Elaboration

Teacher	Children
1. Say: "Now let's try the new patterns we've learned on our sticks! When I call your name, please come and take two sticks from the box. Then go back to your place. Be sure to have enough 'elbow room' for you *and* your sticks." • Demonstrate needed space for sticks to extend and "turn out." • Distribute sticks: call children by name, two at a time, to take their own two sticks.	1. Listen, take sticks.
2. Teacher: Say: "Let's play our Mozart Mouse pattern. Listen first, then echo after me, One, two, ready? Listen!" • Tap: ♩ ♩ ♩ 𝄽 • Say: Moz - art Mouse, rest (move sticks away from each other on 𝄽)	2. Echo tapping pattern: ♩ ♩ ♩ 𝄽
3. Choose individual children to play the echo pattern. Class echoes each pattern.	3. Echo patterns with rhythm sticks.
4. Say: "When I say your name, come to the center and put your sticks in the box."	4. Listen, return sticks to the box.
5. Say: "Now we're going to hear some music that has our pattern! Let's walk in a circle, then freeze when it rests." • Play *Mexican Hat Dance* (CD **26**).	5. Walk and freeze.

Part 5: Closing

Teacher	Children
1. Pass out crayons and copies of **Quiet, Please!** coloring sheet, page 102. • Play Beethoven's *Symphony No. 5 in C Minor* (CD **27**) while children color.	1. Color **Quiet, Please!** coloring sheet.
2. Say: "Now it's time for us to sing goodbye to our music friends, Mozart Mouse and Beethoven Bear." • Sing the *Goodbye Song* (CD **30**). (See page 22 for lyrics.)	2. Sing and do movements.

Ideas for Connections in the Music Center

1. Social/Language/Imagination

a. Emphasize pantomime to represent silence. White gloves can be used for a mime type of activity.

b. Encourage children to use gestures rather than words to communicate. Use some American Sign Language examples for simple cues.

2. Musical Ideas

Play one of the two rhythm patterns from class, using percussion instruments.

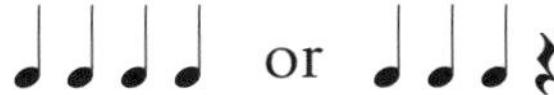

3. Musical/Representational

a. Place in the Music Center simple cards or blocks with individual quarter notes and individual quarter rests. Encourage children to create rhythm patterns from them.

b. Ask each child to write his/her name on a blank card. Does it match the ♩♩♩♩ or ♩♩♩𝄽 patterns? Make a chart of children's names that match each pattern.

4. Other

Read books that explore signs and silence, such as:

A Quiet Night In, by Jill Murphy, Candlewick Press, 1998.

Good Dog, Carl, by Alexandra Day, Little Simon, 1996.

An Alphabet of Animal Signs, by S. Harold Collins, Kathy Kifer and Donna Solar, Garlic Press, 2001.

The Snowman, by Raymond Briggs, Random House Books for Young Readers, 1978.

Lesson 9

Building with Patterns

Musical Concept Emphasis: Rhythm Patterns (♩ ♩ ♩ ♩ and ♩ ♩ ♩ 𝄽)

Teaching Materials

- ❑ *Classroom Music for Little Mozarts* CD 💿
- ❑ CD player
- ❑ *Classroom Music for Little Mozarts* Big Music Book, pages 20–21:

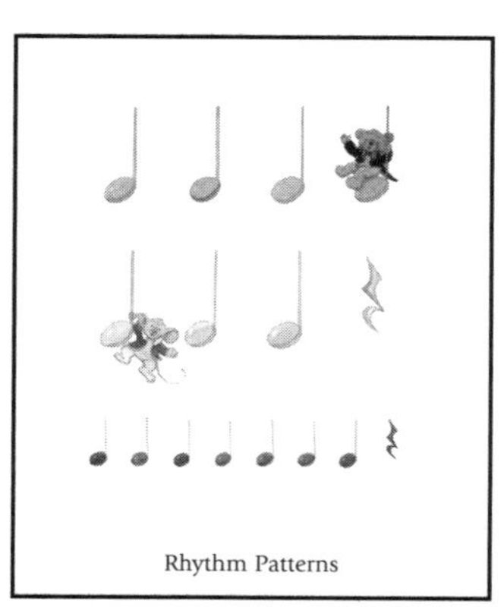

- ❑ Mozart Mouse, Beethoven Bear and Clara Schumann-Cat plush animals
- ❑ Rhythm sticks, 1 pair for each student
- ❑ Crayons for each student
- ❑ Coloring sheet: copies of page 103 for each student:

Lesson 9 Overview

Part 1: Introduction
- *Hello Song* (💿1)

Part 2: Story Connections (Big Music Book, page 20)
- **Chapter 9—Building with Patterns (💿28)**

Part 3: Visual Representation (Big Music Book, page 21)

Review fast/slow, loud/soft, high/low.
Echo ♩ ♩ ♩ 𝄽 rhythm with sticks.
- *Mexican Hat Dance* (💿26)
  Play sticks.
- Echo rhythm on sticks: ♩ ♩ ♩ ♩ ♩ ♩ ♩ 𝄽
- *Mozart Mouse's Song* (💿25)
  Sing, play sticks.

Part 4: Extension and Elaboration
- Big Music Book (page 21), *Twinkle, Twinkle, Little Star* rhythm combination
  a) Say words, point to rhythm.
  b) Add movement.
- Match word syllables to rhythm patterns:

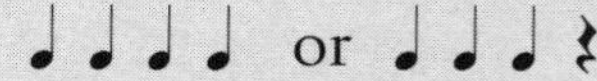

Part 5: Closing
- Color page 103 while listening to *Mexican Hat Dance* (💿26).
- *Goodbye Song* (💿30)

Part 1: Introduction and Review

Teacher	Children
Sing *Hello Song* (💿1) with movements. (See page 17 for lyrics.)	Stand, sing and imitate teacher's motions.

Part 2: Story Connections

Teacher	Children
Say: "Let's find out what our music friends Mozart Mouse and Beethoven Bear are doing this week. Mozart Mouse discovered something very special about his name when we read our story last time. The pattern of his name has the symbol for silence in it—the quarter rest. It sounds like this: Mo-zart-Mouse, *shh*. Our music friends now know two rhythm patterns (♩ ♩ ♩ ♩ and ♩ ♩ ♩ 𝄽). Let's find out what they are going to do with them." • Show Big Music Book, page 20. • Read aloud **Chapter 9—Building With Patterns** (💿28).	Sit, watch and listen.

28

Chapter 9: Building with Patterns

All day long, Mozart Mouse and Beethoven Bear let the children play musical games with them. When the children and teacher had left the classroom for the day, Mozart Mouse and Beethoven Bear decided to play with some of the toys. They went to the Play Center to see what they could find.

"Look at these blocks!" Mozart Mouse exclaimed. "Some have quarter *notes* on them and some have quarter *rests* on them."

Beethoven Bear ran over to see what he was talking about. "Let's put them together to make the rhythm patterns we heard at music time," he suggested. It took some work, but they soon had the blocks arranged in a pattern of four quarter notes. Next, they arranged a pattern of three quarter notes and one quarter rest.

Mozart Mouse stopped and thought for a moment. "Let's see what happens if we put the two patterns together." They were puffing by the time they were finished. They tapped the combined patterns and looked at each other proudly. "We should leave this here until tomorrow and show Clara what we have done," Beethoven Bear suggested.

"That's a good idea," said Mozart Mouse.

They both sat on the floor to rest. "Whew," sighed Beethoven Bear. "Moving blocks is hard work." Just then, he felt a familiar rumble in his tummy. "I'm hungry," he said. "Let's eat."

After a yummy dinner of cheese sticks and peanut butter and honey sandwiches, Mozart Mouse and Beethoven Bear sat in their living room drinking tea.

Mozart Mouse had been thinking. "Do you know what we can call ourselves now that we can put together our own rhythm patterns?"

"Tired?" Beethoven Bear said with a smile.

"No, silly! We're composers. Composers put sounds and rhythms together, and that's just what we did with the blocks this afternoon."

"Maybe we'll be famous composers," Beethoven Bear suggested.

"Or maybe we'll meet a famous composer some day," Mozart Mouse added. "Perhaps Clara Schumann-Cat knows some famous composers. After all, her great-grandmother knew several. We'll have to ask her sometime. "

Beethoven Bear yawned. "Let's go to bed now so we won't be late for our music lesson tomorrow. I can't wait to show Clara what we did today."

The next morning, Beethoven Bear and Mozart Mouse showed Clara Schumann-Cat what they had done with the blocks.

Clara purred with satisfaction and said, "You both have learned so much, I think that it's time to share your music with some of your other friends. I want you to give a concert."

"A concert? Really?" Mozart Mouse asked.

"Yes," Clara answered, "who would you like to invite?"

"Let's invite our friends from the Play Center," Beethoven Bear suggested. "There's J. S. Bunny, Nina Ballerina, Elgar E. Elephant. . ." he began.

"And don't forget Pachelbel Penguin and Puccini Pooch," Mozart Mouse added.

"It sounds like you have a lot of friends," Clara said. "Now let's decide what music you are going to perform."

They spent the rest of the morning choosing the music for the concert and practicing their pieces. They were going to sing songs that Clara had taught them and songs they had learned from listening to the children's music class. Next, they went to the Art Center and made a big poster listing all of the songs that would be on the program. They were quite proud of the way it looked! Then, they made the invitations, took them to the Play Center and gave them to their friends. Finally, they went home early so they could get a good night's sleep. The concert was the next afternoon!

Part 3: Visual Representation

Teacher	Children
1. Say: "Mozart Mouse and Beethoven Bear practiced their music. We're going to practice in our lesson today as well." • Review Big Music Book, page 13: fast/slow, loud/soft, high/low.	1. Sit, listen.
2. Say: "When I call your name, please come to the box, take a pair of sticks, and go back to your place."	2. Sit, follow directions.
3. Say: "Listen and echo what I play." ♩ ♩ ♩ 𝄽 ♩ ♩ ♩ 𝄽 "This is the rhythm we will play in our next song."	3. Sit, echo rhythm, answer question.
4. Play *Mexican Hat Dance* (💿26). (See piano arrangement, pages 126–127.) • Play sticks with recording.	4. Sit, play sticks.
5. Review the rhythm pattern for *Mozart Mouse's Song* (Big Music Book, page 21). Play on rhythm sticks and say: ♩ ♩ ♩ 𝄽 ♩ ♩ ♩ 𝄽 Moz - art Mouse said, "Oh, please"	5. Sit, echo tapping pattern with rhythm sticks.
6. Say: "You are such good listeners! You know just when to have silence, and when to have sound. This time let's try another pattern. For this one you'll have to listen for a longer time. Be careful!" • Point to the rhythms in the Big Music Book chart (page 21) as you play on rhythm sticks and say: ♩ ♩ ♩ ♩ ♩ ♩ ♩ 𝄽 "will - you sing a song with me?"	6. Sit, echo tapping pattern with rhythm sticks.
7. Sing *Mozart Mouse's Song* (💿25). (See page 63 for lyrics.) • Point to the rhythms in the Big Music Book chart (page 21) as you sing and tap. ♩ ♩ ♩ 𝄽 ♩ ♩ ♩ 𝄽 Moz - art Mouse said, "Oh, please ♩ ♩ ♩ ♩ ♩ ♩ ♩ 𝄽 will you sing a song with me? ♩ ♩ ♩ 𝄽 ♩ ♩ ♩ 𝄽 I have friends, here to play. ♩ ♩ ♩ ♩ ♩ ♩ ♩ 𝄽 We will have a mu - sic day."	7. Sit, sing, and tap rhythms for song.
8. Say: "That was such good playing! When I say your name, please return your sticks to the box.	8. Sit, follow directions.

Part 4: Extension and Elaboration

Teacher

1. Show students the rhythm to *Twinkle, Twinkle, Little Star* (Big Music Book, page 21).
   - Say the words "Twinkle, twinkle, little star," and point to the rhythm in the Big Music Book.

     Twin - kle, twin - kle, lit - tle star

   - Say: "Let's clap the rhythm for *Twinkle, Twinkle, Little Star* as we say the words.
2. Stand, sing *Twinkle, Twinkle, Little Star* (piano arrangement, page 119) without the CD.
   - Add the movement of one large step forward on beats one and three of the patterns. (Step on the bold parts of the words.)

     Twin-kle, **twin**-kle, **lit**-tle **star, how** I **won**-der **what** you **are!**
     Up a-**bove** the **world** so **high, like** a **dia**-mond **in** the **sky.**
     Twin-kle, **twin**-kle, **lit**-tle **star, How** I **won**-der **what** you **are!**
3. Say: "Let's find some other words to match our patterns."
   - Match the following words and phrases to the first pattern or the second pattern in the Big Music Book (page 21).
   - Say: "Which pattern goes with each word? Say each word after me."

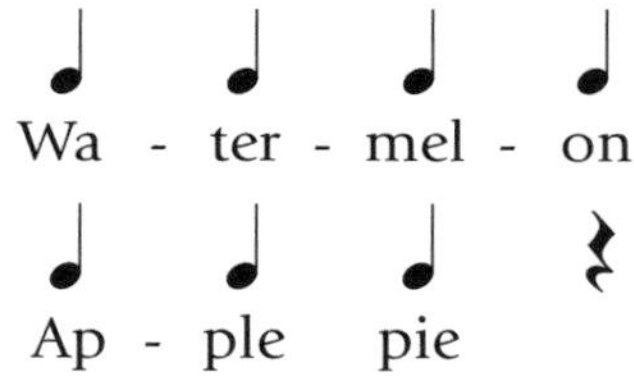

Ka - te - ri - na

Josh - u - a

(Use three- and four-syllable names from the class.)

Optional Put the three- and four-syllable names together to make longer patterns:

Children

1. Sit, watch, listen, clap and say words.
2. Stand, sing, follow teacher's instructions.
3. Sit, listen, answer questions.

Part 5: Closing

Teacher	Children
1. Pass out crayons and copies of **Building with Patterns** coloring sheet, page 103. • Play *Mexican Hat Dance* (CD **26**) while children color.	1. Color **Building with Patterns** coloring sheet.
2. Say: "Now it's time for us to sing goodbye to our music friends, Mozart Mouse and Beethoven Bear." • Sing the *Goodbye Song* (CD **30**). (See page 22 for lyrics.)	2. Sing and do movements.

Ideas for Connections in the Music Center

1. Social/Language/Imagination

a. Children can use pages of musical notation (old sheet music or choral music) and pretend to read the music.

b. Children can pretend to be Wolfgang Amadeus Mozart or Ludwig van Beethoven and write music.

2. Musical Ideas

Children can create their own musical "score" by cutting and pasting parts from old sheet music into a new personal "composition."

3. Musical/Representational

In the Music Center, place cards or blocks with the two notation patterns they have learned (♩ ♩ ♩ ♩ and ♩ ♩ ♩ 𝄽). Children can combine the patterns and play them on instruments.

4. Other—Reading

Read a book that explores musical themes, such as:

The Happy Hedgehog Band, by Martin Waddell and Jill Barton, Pearson Learning, 1992.

Lesson 10

Sharing with Friends

Musical Concept Emphasis: Review/Program

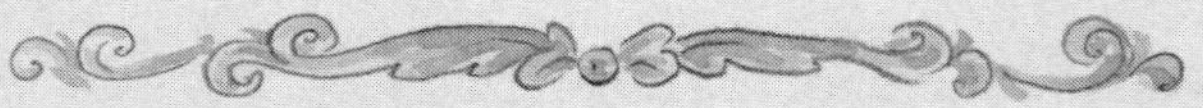

Teaching Materials

- ❑ *Classroom Music for Little Mozarts* CD
- ❑ CD player
- ❑ *Classroom Music for Little Mozarts* Big Music Book, pages 22–24:

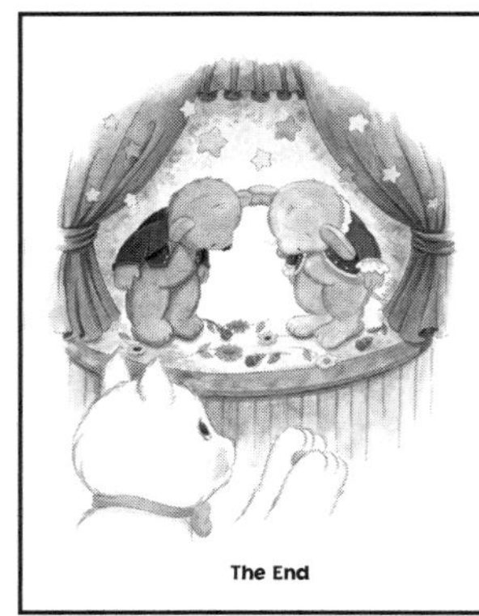

- ❑ Mozart Mouse, Beethoven Bear and Clara Schumann-Cat plush animals
- ❑ (Optional) Rhythm sticks, 1 pair for each student
- ❑ (Optional) Shakers, 1 for each student
- ❑ Coloring sheet: copies of page 104 for each student:

- ❑ Crayons for each student

Lesson 10 Overview

Part 1: Introduction
- *Hello Song* (1)

Part 2: Visual Representation (Big Music Book, page 22)
- Discuss pictures of Mozart Mouse and Beethoven Bear.

Part 3: Story Connections and Program* (Big Music Book, page 23)
- **Chapter 10—Sharing with Friends (29)**
  Songs to be selected from:
  Do, Re, Mi Tapping Song (19)
  The Itsy Bitsy Spider (7)
  Johnny Works with One Hammer (20)
  Mozart Mouse's Song (25)
  The Old Gray Cat (14)
  Racing Car (8)
  Twinkle, Twinkle, Little Star (16)

Part 4: Closing
- Color page 104 while listening to Mozart's *Variations on Twinkle, Twinkle, Little Star* (17).
- *Goodbye Song* (30)

***Note to Teacher:** A copy of your program may be displayed in the space provided in the Big Music Book, page 23.

Part 1: Introduction and Review

Teacher	Children
Sing *Hello Song* (CD 1) with movements. (See page 17 for lyrics.)	Stand, sing and imitate teacher's motions.

Part 2: Visual Representation

Teacher	Children
Show picture in the Big Music Book, page 22. • Ask: "What are Mozart Mouse and Beethoven Bear doing in the picture?" *[performing their concert]*	Sit, answer question.

Part 3: Story Connections and Program

Teacher	Children
(Trim your performance program and insert on page 23 of Big Music Book.) Say: "Last week, Mozart Mouse and Beethoven Bear were planning their concert. Let's listen to see how their plans are going." Show Big Music Book, page 23. • Read aloud **Chapter 10—Sharing with Friends** (CD 29).	Sit, listen, perform.

29

Chapter 10: Sharing with Friends

When they arrived at the Music Center the next day, Clara had a special surprise for them. She had added to the top of their poster the heading "Beethoven Bear and Mozart Mouse Present Songs from Their Musical Adventures." It was the perfect way to describe what their lessons had been like.

Their adventures had included playing high and low, up and down, fast and slow, and loud and soft sounds on the instruments in the Music Center. They had met a wonderful cat named Clara Schumann-Cat. She had become their friend, teaching them many things about music, including quarter notes and quarter rests. They had also learned songs that the class sang and other ones that Clara Schumann-Cat sang to them.

Mozart Mouse and Beethoven Bear were very excited about sharing these songs with their friends. They were ready for the concert to begin!

Program

Teacher should select songs from the following for the students to perform:

Do, Re, Mi Tapping Song (19)

The Itsy Bitsy Spider (7)

Johnny Works With One Hammer (20)

Mozart Mouse's Song (25)

The Old Gray Cat (14)

Racing Car (8)

Twinkle, Twinkle, Little Star (16)

At the end of the concert, Mozart Mouse and Beethoven Bear stood in front of their friends who were clapping loudly. They took a bow and smiled. Clara Schumann-Cat congratulated them on their fine job. *(Show page 24 of Big Music Book.)*

Mozart Mouse looked at Clara and said, "Thank you, Clara for all that you have taught us." Then he looked at his friend. He was surprised that Beethoven Bear looked a little sad.

"What's wrong?" Mozart Mouse asked him anxiously.

"I was just wondering. . ." Beethoven Bear said, hesitating. "Do you think our musical adventures are over?"

"Oh, no," Clara purred in a reassuring voice, "I think that they are just beginning."

Beethoven Bear's face lit up with a big grin. "You do?" he cried. "Why don't we start a new adventure right now!"

So the three friends walked over to the Big Music Book, opened it up and turned to a new page. They were ready for their next musical adventure.

THE END

Part 4: Closing

Teacher	Children
1. Pass out crayons and copies of **Sharing with Friends** coloring sheet, page 104. • Play Mozart's *Variations on Twinkle, Twinkle, Little Star* (💿 **17**) while children color.	1. Color **Sharing with Friends** coloring sheet.
2. Say: "Now it's time for us to sing goodbye to our music friends, Mozart Mouse and Beethoven Bear." • Sing the *Goodbye Song* (💿 **30**). (See page 22 for lyrics.)	2. Sing and do movements.

Ideas for Connections in the Music Center

1. Social/Language/Imagination

Pretend to give a concert. There is a need for cooperative play to have a concert with every student having a role. Encourage some students to use a stick as a conductor's baton. Others may dress like Beethoven Bear and Mozart Mouse and perform. Set up a special seating area for the concert (chairs or rug squares).

2. Musical Ideas

Pretend to conduct a recording such as Beethoven's *Symphony No. 5 in C Minor.*

3. Musical/Representational

Continue to develop ideas from activities in lessons 6–9 in this category.

4. Other

a. Ask questions to encourage students to think about concerts. Such questions include: Who goes to a concert? Where are concerts held? Could you go to a concert?

b. Read books that explore concerts and recitals, such as:

The Philharmonic Gets Dressed, by Karla Kuskin, Harper Trophy, 1986.

Moses Goes to a Concert, by Isaac Millman. Sunburst, 2002.

Henry the Steinway and the Piano Recital, by Sally Coveleskie and Peter Goodrich, Bright Sky Press, 2002.

Appendix A: Student Assessment

Teachers should assess the students' musical behaviors at least once during the ten-week program. This assessment should result from repeated observations over the course of the ten-week program, in four categories:

1) vocal behaviors (singing),
2) playing instruments,
3) moving expressively and rhythmically to music (movement),
4) creating and representing music (creative behaviors).

After week nine, the teacher should complete the Music Behaviors Checklist that follows, by simply checking behavior exhibited by the child under each category. This assessment should be based on the child's behavior in both the music class as well as individual musical play in the classroom. It can be used for internal assessment only, or adapted as a "report card" to give to parents.

Classroom Music for Little Mozarts
Musical Behaviors Checklist

Student Name ____ Date ____________________

Place a check before each statement that describes the musical behavior of the child.

Vocal Behaviors

- ❑ Child is not yet vocally expressive.
- ❑ Child uses voice expressively in unpitched speech.
- ❑ Child sings two- and three-note tonal patterns accurately within a limited vocal range (D′ to A′).
- ❑ Child sings an entire phrase with accurate pitch.
- ❑ Child sings an entire song with accurate pitch.

Moving Expressively and Rhythmically to Music

- ❑ Child does not yet move to music.
- ❑ Child responds to music through gross motor movements.
- ❑ Child imitates choreographed movements to music.
- ❑ Child creates movements to correlate with contrasts in the expressive qualities of the music.
- ❑ Child creates movements to correlate with contrasts in the rhythmic qualities of the music.

Playing Instruments

- ❑ Child does not yet play instruments.
- ❑ Child plays instruments to create sound effects or add tone color to activity.
- ❑ Child plays instruments with steady beat.
- ❑ Child plays rhythmic or tonal patterns using instruments.
- ❑ Child plays extended musical phrases using instruments.

Creating and Representing Music

- ❑ Child does not yet create music.
- ❑ Child creates personal songs to accompany play.
- ❑ Child uses body and props to interpret music.
- ❑ Child creates instrumental accompaniments to songs, recordings, stories, or poems.
- ❑ Child creates short compositions using voices, instruments or other sound sources.
- ❑ Child uses graphic symbols or notation to represent musical ideas.

Appendix B: CD Track List

The compact disc recording supports the concepts introduced in the *Classroom Music for Little Mozarts* curriculum. The disc includes the narration of the story, and professional performances of the listening examples, songs, and movement activities. Each example on the CD is identified by an icon ( ) in the lessons, followed by the track number.

Track	Title
1	*Hello Song* (pages 106–107*)
2	Lesson 1 Story: **New Music Friends** (pages 18, 79**)
3	*High and Low Song* (pages 108–109)
4	*If You're Happy and You Know It* (page 110)
5	*Do You Know?* (page 111)
6	Lesson 2 Story: **Moving to Music** (pages 26, 79–80)
7	*The Itsy Bitsy Spider* (pages 112–113)
8	*Racing Car* (page 114)
9	Lesson 3 Story: **Sound and More Sound** (pages 32–33, 80–81)
10	*Giant's Lullaby* (page 115)
11	Ludwig van Beethoven's *Rage Over the Lost Penny*
12	Franz Joseph Haydn's *Surprise Symphony*
13	Lesson 4 Story: **Speed Limits** (pages 37, 81)
14	*The Old Gray Cat* (pages 116–118)
15	Lesson 5 Story: **Try This!** (pages 42–43, 81–82)
16	*Twinkle, Twinkle, Little Star* (page 119)
17	Wolfgang Amadeus Mozart's *Variations on Twinkle, Twinkle, Little Star*
18	Lesson 6 Story: **Get That Beat!** (pages 48–49, 82–83)
19	*Do, Re, Mi Tapping Song* (pages 120–121)
20	*Johnny Works With One Hammer* (pages 121–123)
21	John Philip Sousa's *Stars and Stripes Forever*
22	Lesson 7 Story: **Music Signs** (pages 56, 83)
23	Johann Sebastian Bach's *Musette in D*
24	Lesson 8 Story: **Quiet, Please!** (pages 62, 83–84)
25	*Mozart Mouse's Song* (pages 124–125)
26	*Mexican Hat Dance* (pages 126–127)
27	Ludwig van Beethoven's *Symphony No. 5 in C Minor*
28	Lesson 9 Story: **Building With Patterns** (pages 68–69, 84–85)
29	Lesson 10 Story: **Sharing With Friends** (pages 74, 85–86)
30	*Goodbye Song* (page 128)

*Piano Arrangement page numbers

**Story page numbers

Appendix C: Complete Story

The Musical Adventures of Beethoven Bear and Mozart Mouse

Chapter 1: New Music Friends 2

Once upon a time, there was a school where children just about your age went every day. In that school, there was a wonderful classroom filled with all sorts of things to help the children learn. There was a big white board to write on, colorful bulletin boards with artwork, shelves filled with books to read, crayons and markers for drawing, tables where the children did their work, a Play Center filled with lots of toys, and even a Music Center with many musical instruments. But of all the things the children had in their classroom, their favorites were a little stuffed bear and a little stuffed mouse. Their names were Beethoven Bear and Mozart Mouse.

All day long, Beethoven Bear and Mozart Mouse sat quietly in the classroom, allowing the children to play with them during free time. But at night, Beethoven Bear and Mozart Mouse did something quite different! When the children went home and the teacher had locked the door, the little bear and little mouse would quickly turn on the lights and hurry from the little house in the Play Center where they lived, to their favorite place in the classroom—the Music Center. They spent many hours happily playing with the instruments.

One evening while they were playing, they discovered that some of the instruments made high sounds, and some made low sounds. Beethoven Bear said to Mozart Mouse, "I love to play low sounds!"

Mozart Mouse replied, "I think high sounds are the best!"

"No!" Beethoven Bear said, "Low sounds are better. They are perfect for a bear like me."

"No!" Mozart Mouse would reply. "The high sounds are perfect for a mouse like me."

And so went the conversation that Beethoven Bear and Mozart Mouse had many times when they played in the Music Center. Sometimes they would take a peek in the Big Music Book that the teacher always used in class. "This must be a really special book," said Beethoven Bear. Mozart Mouse added, "The children learn so many wonderful things from this book."

Beethoven Bear and Mozart Mouse invite you to join them in their musical adventures. They are your new music friends, and together they will take you on a journey through the exciting world of music.

Chapter 2: Moving to Music 6

One evening, Beethoven Bear and Mozart Mouse were playing in the Music Center as usual. Beethoven Bear was playing low sounds, and Mozart Mouse was playing high sounds. As they were playing, they noticed something different about the xylophone. "Look!" Mozart Mouse said to his friend. "The xylophone is leaning against the wood block, and it looks almost like stairs. I'm going to climb it." And with that, Mozart Mouse began to climb the xylophone.

"Hey!" Beethoven Bear exclaimed. "Did you hear what happened to the sound?" He was certain that he had just made an important discovery. "It started low and got higher as you climbed up. I want to try that, too."

Beethoven Bear scurried up the instrument to join his friend at the top. "I've never seen the classroom from up here before," Beethoven Bear remarked. They stood quietly, admiring the view. Then suddenly, they heard a noise!

"What is that?" Beethoven Bear whispered to Mozart Mouse. "Quick!" Mozart Mouse advised his friend. "Slide down the xylophone and hide."

The sound that came from sliding down the xylophone made them giggle. "That was fun!" Beethoven Bear squealed with delight. "Shh," Mozart Mouse warned. "I think someone is coming in."

The two friends huddled together behind the instruments, wondering what would happen next.

Chapter 3: Sound and More Sound 9

The key turned in the lock, and someone opened the door to the classroom. Mozart Mouse peeked out from behind the big drum where he and Beethoven Bear were hiding. He let out a sigh of relief.

"It's only the teacher, Ms. Tina," he whispered to Beethoven Bear. He and Beethoven Bear went to the Music Center every day to listen as she taught music to the children.

Ms. Tina walked over to the Music Center. She opened up the Big Music Book. As she looked at the book, she began to play a few of the instruments one at a time. Some of the instruments made soft sounds and some of them made loud sounds. Mozart Mouse liked to hear her play.

"I think she's planning tomorrow's music lesson," Mozart Mouse reported to his friend. Soon, Ms. Tina finished. She closed the book and walked to the door. After turning off the lights, she closed the door behind her and locked it. Beethoven Bear and Mozart Mouse had learned to listen for the sound of the key in the lock. It meant that they were free to play for the rest of the evening without any interruptions.

The first thing Beethoven Bear did was find the drums. He began to play as loudly as he could.

"Hey! You'd better be quiet!" Mozart Mouse cautioned his friend. "Ms. Tina might hear us."

"Oops," said Beethoven Bear, "I was having so much fun, I forgot!"

"Why don't you play something with a soft sound like this?" Mozart Mouse suggested as he picked up the triangle and struck it lightly. He handed the triangle to Beethoven Bear, who began to play it quietly.

Mozart Mouse had other plans that evening. Earlier in the day, he had heard the children singing a song about a racing car. He couldn't wait to drive the little red toy car that the children loved to race around the room. Soon, Mozart Mouse was zooming in and out between the tables and chairs in the classroom.

"I feel just like a race car driver!" he thought to himself.

He looked at the clock on the classroom wall and came to a screeching halt beside Beethoven Bear. "Time for bed, my friend," he said. "Hop in, and I'll give you a ride home."

Mozart Mouse parked the car next to the little house. The two friends got out and climbed the stairs to the second floor where their cozy beds were waiting for them. As they snuggled under the covers, Mozart Mouse began to hum a quiet lullaby to his friend.

"Goodnight," Mozart Mouse whispered to Beethoven Bear when he was finished. But Beethoven Bear was already fast asleep, dreaming about the adventures that they would have the next day.

Chapter 4: Speed Limits 13

The next morning, Mozart Mouse lay in bed with his eyes closed. He thought he heard singing. It was a song about a cat. For a moment, he forgot where he was. Then he sat up and sneezed, "Ah-choo!"

"Oh, dear," he thought to himself. "I hope there isn't a cat in the room. I am very allergic to cats." Then, he looked at the clock on the nightstand. It was already 9:00 a.m. He and Beethoven Bear had overslept! The singing he heard was coming from the Music Center. The children had already started their music lesson for the day!

He jumped out of bed and went over to wake up Beethoven Bear.

"We've got to hurry," he urged his friend. "We might miss something important."

They ran quickly down the stairs and climbed into the toy racing car. Mozart Mouse drove as fast as he could to the other side of the room. It wasn't easy, because the children had scattered toys all over the floor. It looked like an obstacle course as he drove in and out.

"Slow down!" Beethoven Bear urged. "You are driving too fast!"

Suddenly, something large loomed ahead of them. From out of nowhere, a big, white, furry ball appeared. Mozart Mouse stepped on the brakes. Beethoven Bear covered his eyes. It looked as if they were going to run into a giant cotton ball!

The little red racing car went slower and slower until it finally came to a stop. Beethoven Bear opened his eyes. What he thought was a giant cotton ball was, in fact, a beautiful white cat.

Chapter 5: Try This! 15

Beethoven Bear and Mozart Mouse sat in the car, too terrified to speak. They had almost run into the beautiful white cat!

"I beg your pardon," the cat purred. "You seem to be in quite a hurry. Is there a problem?"

Mozart Mouse cleared his throat nervously and spoke. "Please excuse us! We are late for music time," he looked around the room and continued, "but there were quite a few toys in our way."

"Allow me to help you," the cat offered. "Climb on my back, and I will take you to the Music Center."

Mozart Mouse wasn't at all sure what to do. If he got anywhere near the cat, he was certain he would start sneezing. On the other hand, if he didn't let the cat help them, he and Beethoven Bear would probably miss the music lesson.

"Thank you," he said hesitantly. Then, he got out of the car and climbed up to take a seat on top of the furry cat. Beethoven Bear followed him. They held on tightly as the cat walked slowly toward the children seated in the Music Center.

When they arrived, the two friends slid down to the floor and scrambled to get a good view of what the children were doing.

Ms. Tina was teaching the class a song about an old gray cat. They were singing loud and soft and fast and slow. The Big Music Book was open to a picture of Mozart Mouse and Beethoven Bear going up and down the stairs of the playhouse. *(Show page 7 of Big Music Book.)*

"That's us in the picture!" Beethoven Bear said proudly to the cat.

"Oh, I already know who you are," the cat purred. "You're Beethoven Bear and Mozart Mouse. The children talk about you all the time."

"That's odd," Mozart Mouse thought to himself. "How would this cat know the children?"

He cleared his throat. "If you please, won't you tell us your name?" he asked shyly.

"It would be my pleasure," was the reply, "as soon as the teacher finishes reviewing high and low sounds."

Mozart Mouse was amazed! Who was this cat, and how did she know things about music? And why wasn't he sneezing?

Chapter 6: Get That Beat! 18

Mozart Mouse, Beethoven Bear, and the beautiful white cat watched and listened to the music lesson. When the teacher finished the lesson, the cat turned to them and smiled. "My name is Clara Schumann-Cat," she began. She purred happily as she told Beethoven Bear and Mozart Mouse about her musical background. "Everyone in my family plays the piano," she said proudly. "In fact, my great-grandmother was taught by Clara Schumann herself. Clara Schumann played the piano and composed music. She was very famous, you know. My mother named me after her."

"It's an honor to meet you," Beethoven Bear and Mozart Mouse said. Then Mozart Mouse continued, "We're forgetting our manners. Thank you so much for bringing us to the Music Center. We never would have made it without you. But if you don't mind my asking, what are you doing here in our classroom?"

"Don't you know?" Clara asked with surprise. The two friends shook their heads.

"Why, I am Ms. Tina's cat," she explained. "Sometimes she brings me to school, and I sit quietly and watch everything that happens in class. I'm surprised we never met before."

Just then, a steady hammering sound, *tap, tap, tap, tap,* interrupted their conversation.

"What's that?" Beethoven Bear asked.

"Someone must be doing some hammering in the next room," Clara replied. "The steady beat reminds me of a song. Do you know this?" She started to sing *Johnny Works with One Hammer.*

Mozart Mouse and Beethoven Bear quickly joined in, admiring how Clara had taken the sound of the hammer and quickly turned it into a music lesson. She gave each of them a pair of sticks, and they tapped a steady beat as they sang.

"That was fun!" Beethoven Bear exclaimed. "Can we do it again?"

"I can think of something even better," Mozart Mouse said. He turned to Clara and asked, "You seem to know so much about music. Could you give us music lessons?"

Clara Schumann-Cat was beaming. "I've always wanted to teach!" she exclaimed. "Teaching runs in my family, of course. Why don't we meet in the Music Center every day? We can start tomorrow."

"I can't wait!" Beethoven Bear said as he waved goodbye to Clara. He and Mozart Mouse walked back to their car and got in to drive home. "Tomorrow is going to be a special day," he said to Mozart Mouse.

"This time, I'm going to set my alarm clock," Mozart Mouse said. "We don't want to be late."

Chapter 7: Music Signs 22

Mozart Mouse's alarm clock rang very early the next morning. He and Beethoven Bear dressed quickly, ate breakfast, and drove to the Music Center in the toy car. The clock in the room said that it was only 7:00 a.m. Even the children weren't there yet!

Beethoven Bear picked up a pair of sticks and started tapping. "Doesn't this sound like the steady beat we made yesterday?" he asked. Mozart Mouse got a pair of sticks and joined in. They sang the song that Clara Schumann-Cat had taught them.

When they had finished, they heard a steady beat at the door, *tap, tap, tap, tap.* Mozart Mouse ran to see who it could be. He opened the door just a little so that he could peek out. It was Clara Schumann-Cat. "Hi, Clara. You're early," he greeted her.

"I know," she purred as she walked into the room, "but I just couldn't wait to teach my first music lesson. I could hear your sticks when I was at the door. You have a wonderful steady beat." She walked over to the Big Music Book and opened it. "Please join me over here. I would like to show you something," she said as she turned to the page that she wanted. "Now that you know what a steady beat *feels* and *sounds* like, we can see what a steady beat *looks* like." She pointed to the page and showed them how to tap the pattern. "This pattern is made up of four quarter notes," Clara explained. "Let's play this quarter note pattern again."

Beethoven Bear couldn't believe how easy and fun quarter notes could be. "I could do this all day!" he exclaimed as he ran around the Music Center playing quarter note patterns on all of the instruments.

Clara Schumann-Cat looked at the clock. "Shhh! I think it's time for the children to get here," she said in a whisper. She invited them to join her on the big pillow where they could sit and watch what the children did during music time that day.

To their surprise, the teacher turned to the same page that Clara had showed them in the Big Music Book. Mozart Mouse and Beethoven Bear were thrilled. They spent the rest of the day with Clara on her pillow, quietly singing and tapping quarter note patterns.

Chapter 8: Quiet, Please! 24

Mozart Mouse and Beethoven Bear decided that they should get up early every day and go to the Music Center before the children got to school. One morning they were looking in the Big Music Book at a page with a quarter note pattern. But there was another pattern on the page that they had never seen before.

"What do you suppose this is?" asked Beethoven Bear, pointing to a squiggly line after three quarter notes.

"I don't know," Mozart Mouse answered, "but Clara Schumann-Cat will. She knows *everything.*" He sighed. "Do you think we'll ever know as much as she does?" he asked.

"I sure hope so," Beethoven Bear replied. "I'd like to be a music teacher some day." Then he thought for a moment. "I know one question she might not be able to answer."

"What?" Mozart Mouse asked.

Beethoven Bear giggled and said, "Why don't you ever sneeze when she is around? I thought you were really allergic to cats!"

Mozart Mouse giggled, too. "I am!" he exclaimed. "But I guess I'm not allergic to *musical* cats," he said.

"I hope you're right," Beethoven Bear said earnestly. "I wish Clara would get here soon so that we could find out what this is," he added, looking at the book again.

Just then, they heard a *tap, tap, tap, tap* on the door. "I'll bet that's Clara!" said Mozart Mouse as he ran to open the door. Clara walked into the room, ready to begin her lesson. She called them over to the Big Music Book.

"Oh," she began, "I see that you are on the very page I wanted to talk about today." She showed them the pattern from the song *Johnny Works with One Hammer.* They tapped it together. Then she pointed to the other pattern that had Beethoven Bear and Mozart Mouse puzzled, and said, "The squiggly line means silence. It is a quarter rest."

"*Now* I know what that is!" Beethoven Bear said as he pointed to the end of the pattern.

"Excellent!" said Clara. "Let's read and tap this pattern."

When they had finished, Mozart Mouse had made an exciting discovery. "That is just like the pattern in my name," he announced. "Listen," he said, and he began to chant his name and whisper *shh* after it: "Mo-zart-Mouse, *shh;* Mo-zart-Mouse, *shh.*"

Beethoven Bear was giggling again. "The pattern for your name has a symbol for silence in it—a quarter rest. That must be why mice are so quiet!"

Everyone laughed. Clara Schumann-Cat was pleased. "You both learned our lesson very well today. The patterns you learned have a special music name—they are called rhythm patterns. Would you like to play the new rhythm pattern on some instruments before the children get here?" she asked.

Mozart Mouse and Beethoven Bear ran happily to the instruments. Of course Beethoven Bear chose the big drum because he liked low sounds so much. Mozart Mouse chose the triangle so that he could hear his favorite high sounds. Clara's tail swished back and forth to the beat as the music friends played their new rhythm pattern over and over again.

Chapter 9: Building with Patterns 28

All day long, Mozart Mouse and Beethoven Bear let the children play musical games with them. When the children and teacher had left the classroom for the day, Mozart Mouse and Beethoven Bear decided to play with some of the toys. They went to the Play Center to see what they could find.

"Look at these blocks!" Mozart Mouse exclaimed. "Some have quarter *notes* on them and some have quarter *rests* on them."

Beethoven Bear ran over to see what he was talking about. "Let's put them together to make the rhythm patterns we heard at music time," he suggested. It took some work, but they soon had the blocks arranged in a pattern of four quarter notes. Next, they arranged a pattern of three quarter notes and one quarter rest.

Mozart Mouse stopped and thought for a moment. "Let's see what happens if we put the two patterns together." They were puffing by the time they were finished. They tapped the combined patterns and looked at each other proudly. "We should leave this here until tomorrow and show Clara what we have done," Beethoven Bear suggested.

"That's a good idea," said Mozart Mouse.

They both sat on the floor to rest. "Whew," sighed Beethoven Bear. "Moving blocks is hard work." Just then, he felt a familiar rumble in his tummy. "I'm hungry," he said. "Let's eat."

After a yummy dinner of cheese sticks and peanut butter and honey sandwiches, Mozart Mouse and Beethoven Bear sat in their living room drinking tea.

Mozart Mouse had been thinking. "Do you know what we can call ourselves now that we can put together our own rhythm patterns?"

"Tired?" Beethoven Bear said with a smile.

"No, silly! We're composers. Composers put sounds and rhythms together, and that's just what we did with the blocks this afternoon."

"Maybe we'll be famous composers," Beethoven Bear suggested.

"Or maybe we'll meet a famous composer some day," Mozart Mouse added. "Perhaps Clara Schumann-Cat knows some famous composers. After all, her great-grandmother knew several. We'll have to ask her sometime. "

Beethoven Bear yawned. "Let's go to bed now so we won't be late for our music lesson tomorrow. I can't wait to show Clara what we did today."

The next morning, Beethoven Bear and Mozart Mouse showed Clara Schumann-Cat what they had done with the blocks.

Clara purred with satisfaction and said, "You both have learned so much, I think that it's time to share your music with some of your other friends. I want you to give a concert."

"A concert? Really?" Mozart Mouse asked.

"Yes," Clara answered, "who would you like to invite?"

"Let's invite our friends from the Play Center," Beethoven Bear suggested. "There's J. S. Bunny, Nina Ballerina, Elgar E. Elephant. . ." he began.

"And don't forget Pachelbel Penguin and Puccini Pooch," Mozart Mouse added.

"It sounds like you have a lot of friends," Clara said. "Now let's decide what music you are going to perform."

They spent the rest of the morning choosing the music for the concert and practicing their pieces. They were going to sing songs that Clara had taught them and songs they had learned from listening to the children's music class. Next, they went to the Art Center and made a big poster listing all of the songs that would be on the program. They were quite proud of the way it looked! Then, they made the invitations, took them to the Play Center and gave them to their friends. Finally, they went home early so they could get a good night's sleep. The concert was the next afternoon!

Chapter 10: Sharing with Friends 29

When they arrived at the Music Center the next day, Clara had a special surprise for them. She had added to the top of their poster the heading "Beethoven Bear and Mozart Mouse Present Songs from Their Musical Adventures." It was the perfect way to describe what their lessons had been like.

Their adventures had included playing high and low, up and down, fast and slow, and loud and soft sounds on the instruments in the Music Center. They had met a wonderful cat named Clara Schumann-Cat. She had become their friend, teaching them many things about music, including quarter notes and quarter rests. They had also learned songs that the class sang and other ones that Clara Schumann-Cat sang to them.

Mozart Mouse and Beethoven Bear were very excited about sharing these songs with their friends. They were ready for the concert to begin!

Program

Songs to be selected from:

Do, Re, Mi Tapping Song (19)

The Itsy Bitsy Spider (7)

Johnny Works With One Hammer (20)

Mozart Mouse's Song (25)

The Old Gray Cat (14)

Racing Car (8)

Twinkle, Twinkle, Little Star (16)

At the end of the concert, Mozart Mouse and Beethoven Bear stood in front of their friends who were clapping loudly. They took a bow and smiled. Clara Schumann-Cat congratulated them on their fine job. *(Show page 24 of Big Music Book.)*

Mozart Mouse looked at Clara and said, "Thank you, Clara for all that you have taught us." Then he looked at his friend. He was surprised that Beethoven Bear looked a little sad.

"What's wrong?" Mozart Mouse asked him anxiously.

"I was just wondering. . ." Beethoven Bear said, hesitating. "Do you think our musical adventures are over?"

"Oh, no," Clara purred in a reassuring voice, "I think that they are just beginning."

Beethoven Bear's face lit up with a big grin. "You do?" he cried. "Why don't we start a new adventure right now!"

So the three friends walked over to the Big Music Book, opened it up and turned to a new page. They were ready for their next musical adventure.

THE END

Appendix D: Big Music Book Pages

Lesson 1: New Music Friends, pages 4–5

High and Low

Lesson 2: Moving to Music, pages 6–7

Up and Down

Lesson 3: Sound and More Sound, pages 8–9

Loud and Soft

Lesson 4: Speed Limits, pages 10–11

Fast and Slow

Lesson 5: Try This! pages 12–13

High and Low

Up and Down

Loud and Soft

Fast and Slow

Lesson 6: Get That Beat! pages 14–15

Steady Beat

Lesson 7: Music Signs, pages 16–17

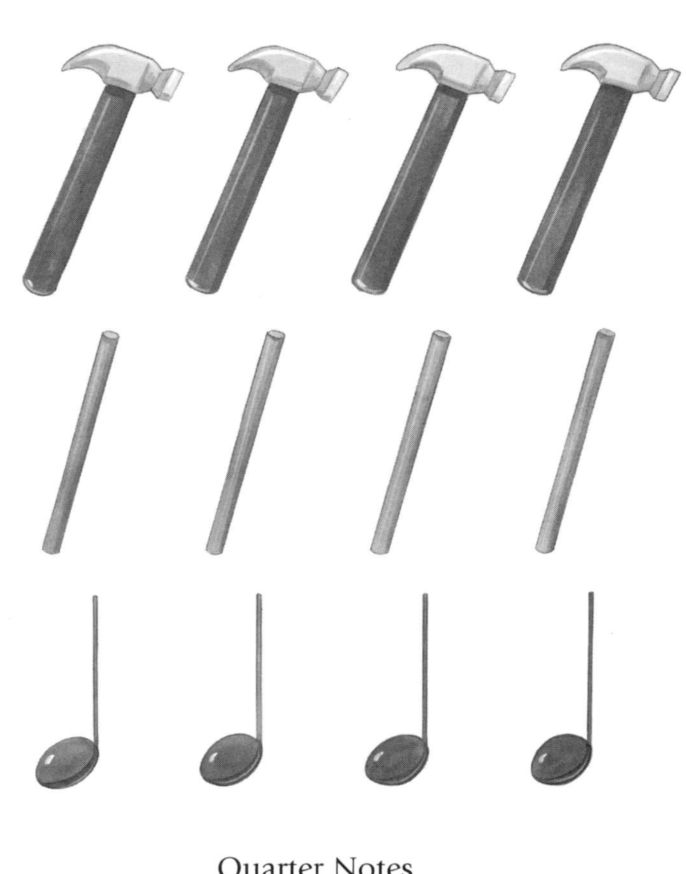

Quarter Notes

Lesson 8: Quiet, Please! pages 18–19

Quarter Rest

Lesson 9: Building with Patterns, pages 20–21

Rhythm Patterns

Lesson 10: Sharing with Friends, pages 22–23

Program

The End

Appendix E: Coloring Pages

Mozart Mouse and Beethoven Bear—our music friends!

Mozart Mouse goes up the blocks.
Beethoven Bear goes down the blocks.

Mozart Mouse makes a loud sound.
Beethoven Bear makes a soft sound.

Lesson 4: Speed Limits

Beethoven Bear and Mozart Mouse drive their racing car fast and slow.

Lesson 5: Try This!

Mozart Mouse and Beethoven Bear sing *Twinkle, Twinkle, Little Star* as they play their shakers.

The music friends march to the beat.

Mozart Mouse and Beethoven Bear learn about quarter notes.

Lesson 8: Quiet, Please!

Mozart Mouse and Beethoven Bear hear this rhythm pattern in *Mexican Hat Dance.*

Lesson 9: Building with Patterns

Clara Schumann-Cat helps Mozart Mouse and Beethoven Bear
combine rhythm patterns.

Mozart Mouse and Beethoven Bear take a bow after their performance.

Appendix F: Piano Arrangements

Hello Song

(It's Music Time Today)

Christine H. Barden

*After the first few lessons, you may begin the *Hello Song* here if so desired.

18
lo, hel-lo, it's mu-sic time to-day. We're glad you're here; it's
LH detached
21
gradually slowing
time to sing and play. We'll clap our hands, (clap) stamp our feet, (stamp)
gradually slowing
24
a tempo
turn a-round, (turn around) touch the ground. (bend down) Hel-lo, hel-lo; it's
a tempo
28
mu-sic time to-day. We're glad you're here; it's time to sing and play.

High and Low Song

Christine H. Barden

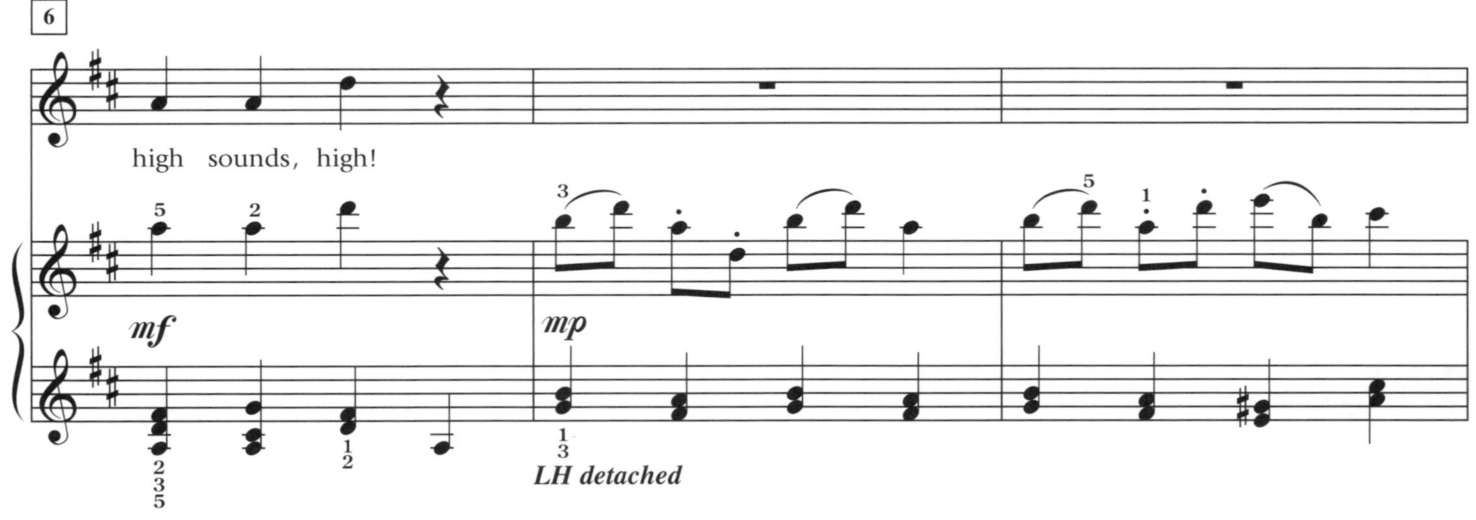

9
8va
cresc.
mf
12
Now, sing low sounds, low sounds, low.
pesante
15
Bee - tho - ven Bear likes low sounds, low!
18
cresc.
f
8va

If You're Happy and You Know It

2. stamp your feet *(stamp feet)*

3. jump up high *(jump high)*

4. do all three *(clap hands, stamp feet, jump high)*

*Teacher plays white key glissando going up and down on the two beats of rest.

Do You Know?

arr. Christine H. Barden
Words by Donna Brink Fox
and Karen Farnum Surmani

The Itsy Bitsy Spider

arr. Christine H. Barden

21
Heavily
mf
The great big spi - der went up the wa - ter spout;
26
f
down came the rain and washed the spi - der out.
Out came the
31
sun and dried up all the rain, and the great big spi - der went
36
mp
up the spout a - gain.
RH
LH

Racing Car

8

Christine H. Barden

*Vocal glissando

Giant's Lullaby

10

The Old Gray Cat

14

arr. Christine H. Barden

21
mp
lit - tle mice are creep - ing in the house. The lit - tle mice are
8va
mp
26
nib - bling, nib - bling, nib - bling. The lit - tle mice are nib - bling
31
Dancing quietly, but faster (♩ = 120)
in the house. The lit - tle mice are danc - ing, danc - ing,
36
danc - ing. The lit - tle mice are danc - ing in the house.
rit.

41
Moderately creeping (♩ = 80)
mf
♩ = ♩.
The old gray cat is
mf
46
creep - ing, creep - ing, creep - ing. The old gray cat is creep - ing
51
Presto (♩ = 144)
mf
in the house. The lit - tle mice are scamp - 'ring, scamp - 'ring,
sfz
mf
56
scamp - 'ring. The lit - tle mice are scamp - 'ring in the house!
8va
cresc. e accel.
f

Twinkle, Twinkle, Little Star

16

arr. Christine H. Barden

Do Re Mi Tapping Song

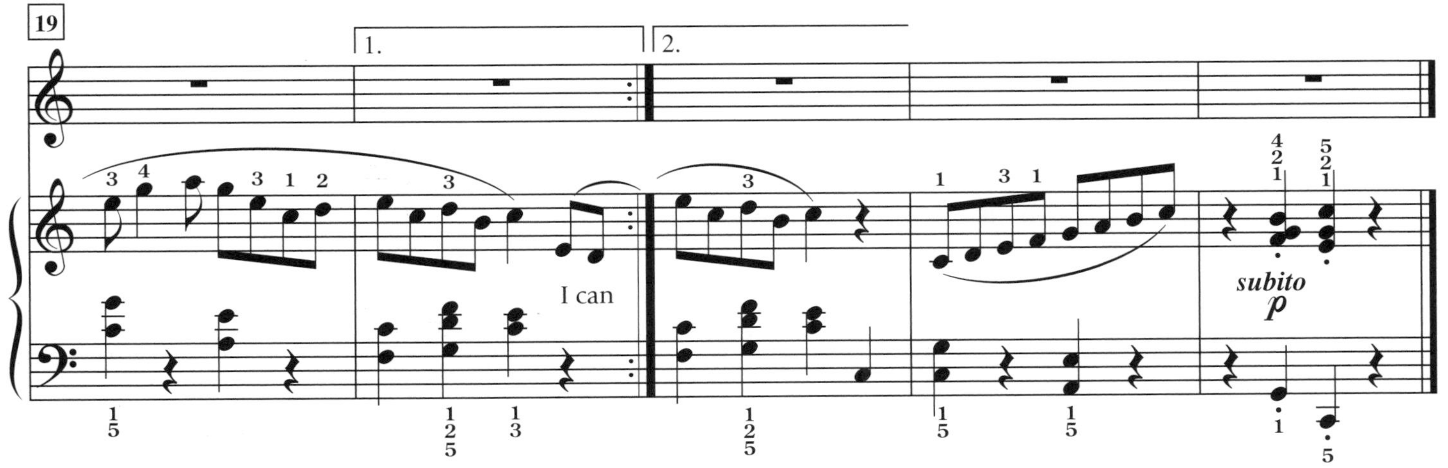

Johnny Works with One Hammer

arr. Christine H. Barden

20

Moderately (♩ = 88)

Tap one fist to each beat, like a hammer.

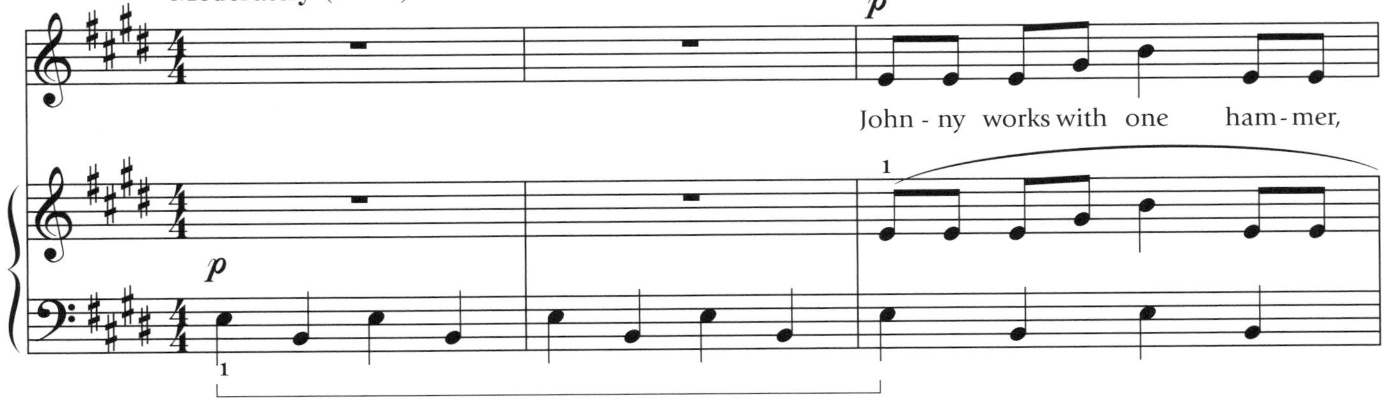

John - ny works with one ham - mer,

4

one ham - mer, one ham - mer, John - ny works with one ham - mer;

6

then he works with two.

9
Add other fist.
mp
John-ny works with two ham-mers, two ham-mers, two ham-mers, John-ny works with two ham-mers;
mp
12
Add one foot.
mf
then he works with three.
John-ny works with three ham-mers,
mf
16
three ham-mers, three ham-mers, John-ny works with three ham-mers; then he works with four.
19
Add other foot.
f
John-ny works with four ham-mers, four ham-mers, four ham-mers,
f

23
John-ny works with four ham-mers; then he works with five.
8va
26
Add head.
ff
John-ny works with five ham-mers, five ham-mers, five ham-mers,
ff
8va
8va
8va
29
5 hammers (2 fists, 2 feet, head)
John-ny works with five ham-mers; then he goes to sleep.
dim. poco a poco
8va
8va
8va
32
4 hammers (2 fists, 2 feet)
3 hammers (2 fists, 1 foot)
2 hammers (2 fists)
1 hammer (1 fist)
zzzzzzzzz
p

Mozart Mouse's Song

25

Christine H. Barden

Playfully (♩ = 120)

mp

5

mp

Mo - zart Mouse said, "Oh, please, will you sing a song with me?

9

I have friends here to play. We will have a mu - sic day."

13
Clap (or play rhythm instruments)
mf
17

Mexican Hat Dance

26

arr. Christine H. Barden

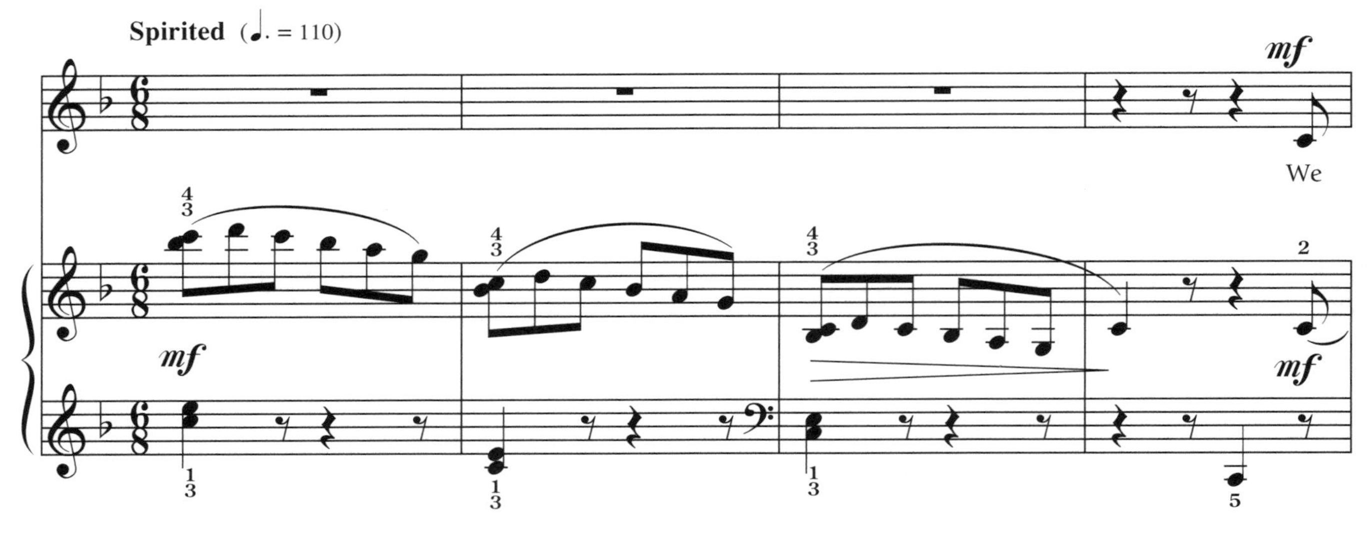

*Note: A quarter note in the student rhythm pattern equals a dotted quarter note in the song.

13
2.
rest.
2.
f

17

21
1.
2.
D. S. al Coda
We
1.
2.
D. S. al Coda
mf

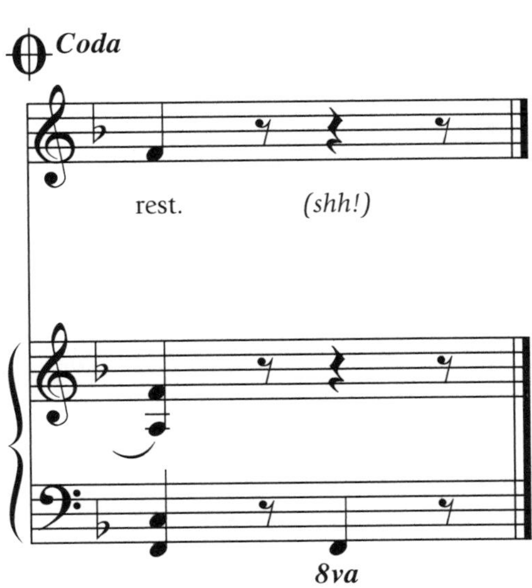
Coda
rest.
(shh!)
8va

Goodbye Song

(It's Time to Say Goodbye)

30

Christine H. Barden

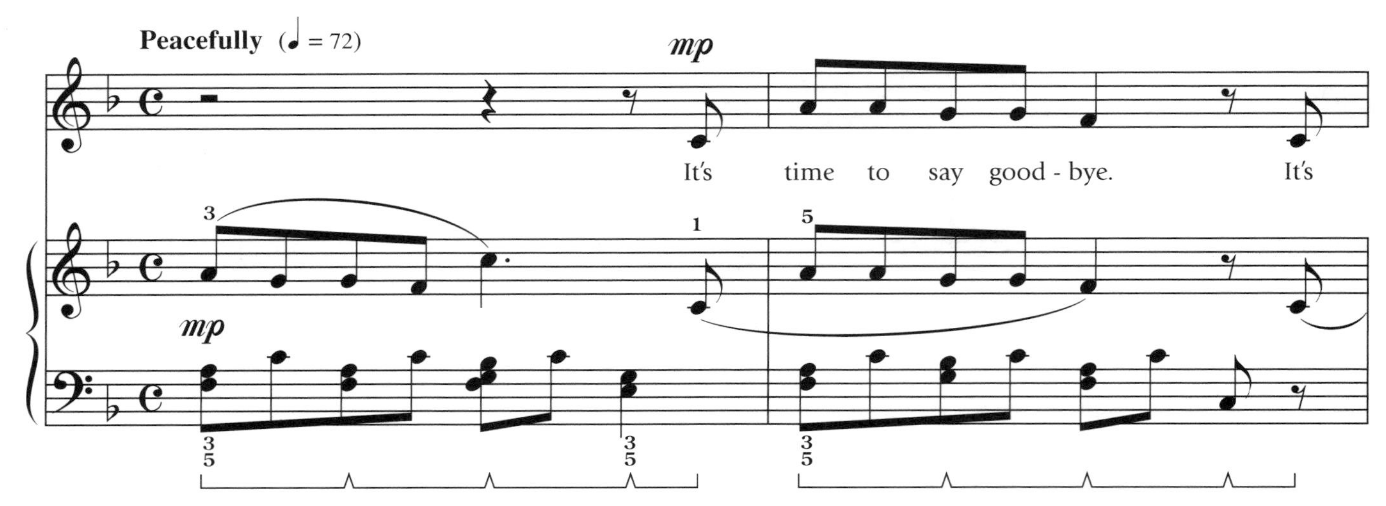

Appendix G: The National Pre-Kindergarten Standards for Music Education (ages 2–4)

1. **Content Standard: Singing and playing instruments**

   Achievement Standard: Children

   a. use their voices expressively as they speak, chant and sing
   b. sing a variety of simple songs in various keys, meters and genres, alone and with a group, becoming increasingly accurate in rhythm and pitch
   c. experiment with a variety of instruments and other sound sources
   d. play simple melodies and accompaniments on instruments

2. **Content Standard: Creating music**

   Achievement Standard: Children

   a. improvise songs to accompany their play activities
   b. improvise instrumental accompaniments to songs, recorded selections, stories and poems
   c. create short pieces of music, using voices, instruments and other sound sources
   d. invent and use original graphic or symbolic systems to represent vocal and instrumental sounds and musical ideas

3. **Content Standard: Responding to music**

   Achievement Standard: Children

   a. identify the sources of a wide variety of sounds
   b. respond through movement to music of various tempos, meters, dynamics, modes, genres, and styles to express what they hear and feel in works of music
   c. participate freely in music

4. **Content Standard: Understanding music**

   Achievement Standard: Children

   a. use their own vocabulary and standard music vocabulary to describe voices, instruments, music notation and music of various genres, styles and periods from diverse cultures
   b. sing, play instruments, move or verbalize to demonstrate awareness of the elements of music and changes in their usage
   c. demonstrate an awareness of music as a part of daily life

Appendix H: The National Standards for Music Education: Grades K–4

1. Content Standard: Singing, alone and with others, a varied repertoire of music

Achievement Standard: Students

a. sing independently, on pitch and in rhythm, with appropriate timbre, diction and posture, and maintain a steady tempo

b. sing expressively, with appropriate dynamics, phrasing and interpretation

c. sing from memory a varied repertoire of songs representing genres and styles from diverse cultures

d. sing ostinatos, partner songs and rounds

e. sing in groups, blending vocal timbres, matching dynamic levels and responding to the cues of a conductor

2. Content Standard: Performing on instruments, alone and with others, a varied repertoire of music

Achievement Standard: Students

a. perform on pitch, in rhythm, with appropriate dynamics and timbre, and maintain a steady tempo

b. perform easy rhythmic, melodic and chordal patterns accurately and independently on rhythmic, melodic and harmonic classroom instruments

c. perform expressively a varied repertoire of music representing diverse genres and styles

d. echo short rhythms and melodic patterns

e. perform in groups, blending instrumental timbres, matching dynamic levels, and responding to the cues of a conductor

f. perform independent instrumental parts while other students sing or play contrasting parts

3. Content Standard: Improvising melodies, variations, and accompaniments

Achievement Standard: Students

a. improvise "answers" in the same style to given rhythmic and melodic phrases

b. improvise simple rhythmic and melodic ostinato accompaniments

c. improvise simple rhythmic variations and simple melodic embellishments on familiar melodies

d. improvise short songs and instrumental pieces, using a variety of sound sources, including traditional sounds, nontraditional sounds available in the classroom, body sounds, and sounds produced by electronic means

4. Content Standard: Composing and arranging music within specified guidelines

Achievement Standard: Students

a. create and arrange music to accompany readings or dramatizations

b. create and arrange short songs and instrumental pieces within specified guidelines

c. use a variety of sound sources when composing

5. Content Standard: Reading and notating music

Achievement Standard: Students

a. read whole, half, dotted half, quarter, and eighth notes and rests in $\frac{2}{4}$, $\frac{3}{4}$, and $\frac{4}{4}$ meter signatures

b. use a system (that is, syllables, numbers, or letters) to read simple pitch notation in the treble clef in major keys

c. identify symbols and traditional terms referring to dynamics, tempo, and articulation and interpret them correctly when performing

d. use standard symbols to notate meter, rhythm, pitch, and dynamics in simple patterns presented by the teacher

6. **Content Standard: Listening to, analyzing, and describing music**

   Achievement Standard: Students

   a. identify simple music forms when presented aurally
   b. demonstrate perceptual skills by moving, by answering questions about, and by describing aural examples of music of various styles representing diverse cultures
   c. use appropriate terminology in explaining music, music notation, music instruments and voices, and music performances
   d. identify the sounds of a variety of instruments, including many orchestra and band instruments, and instruments from various cultures, as well as children's voices and male and female adult voices
   e. respond through purposeful movement to selected prominent music characteristics or to specific music events while listening to music

7. **Content Standard: Evaluating music and music performances**

   Achievement Standard: Students

   a. devise criteria for evaluating performances and compositions
   b. explain, using appropriate music terminology, their personal preferences for specific musical works and styles

8. **Content Standard: Understanding relationships between music, the other arts, and disciplines outside the arts**

   Achievement Standard: Students

   a. identify similarities and differences in the meanings of common terms used in the various arts
   b. identify ways in which the principles and subject matter of other disciplines taught in the school are interrelated with those of music

9. **Content Standard: Understanding music in relation to history and culture**

   Achievement Standard: Students

   a. identify by genre or style aural examples of music from various historical periods and cultures
   b. describe in simple terms how elements of music are used in music examples from various cultures of the world
   c. identify various uses of music in their daily experiences and describe characteristics that make certain music suitable for each use
   d. identify and describe roles of musicians in various music settings and cultures
   e. demonstrate audience behavior appropriate for the context and style of music performed

Index: Songs by Lesson

Sequential Musical Content **(by Lesson)**	Singing	Playing Instruments	Moving to Music	Listening to Music
Lesson 1				
Hello Song 💿1	■		●	
High and Low Song 💿3			●	◆
If You're Happy and You Know It 💿4	■		●	
Do You Know? 💿5	■			◆
Goodbye Song 💿30	■		●	
Lesson 2				
Hello Song 💿1	■		●	
High and Low Song 💿3			●	
The Itsy Bitsy Spider 💿7	■		●	◆
If You're Happy and You Know It 💿4	■		●	
Goodbye Song 💿30	■		●	
Lesson 3				
Hello Song 💿1	■		●	
Racing Car 💿8	■		●	
The Itsy Bitsy Spider 💿7	■		●	
Giant's Lullaby 💿10			●	◆
Beethoven's *Rage Over the Lost Penny* 💿11				◆
Goodbye Song 💿30	■		●	
Lesson 4				
Hello Song 💿1	■		●	
Racing Car 💿8	■		●	
Giant's Lullaby 💿10			●	
The Old Gray Cat 💿14	■		●	◆
Haydn's *Surprise Symphony* 💿12				◆
Goodbye Song 💿30	■		●	

Sequential Musical Content (by Lesson)	Singing	Playing Instruments	Moving to Music	Listening to Music
Lesson 5				
Hello Song 1	■		●	
High and Low Song 3			●	
The Old Gray Cat 14	■		●	
Twinkle, Twinkle, Little Star 16	■	★		
Mozart's Variations on *Twinkle, Twinkle, Little Star* 17				◆
Goodbye Song 30	■		●	
Lesson 6				
Hello Song 1	■		●	
The Old Gray Cat 14	■		●	
Do Re Mi Tapping Song 19	■		●	
Johnny Works with One Hammer 20	■	★	●	
Sousa's *Stars and Stripes Forever* 21				◆
Goodbye Song 30	■		●	
Lesson 7				
Hello Song 1	■		●	
Do Re Mi Tapping Song 19	■		●	
Racing Car 8	■		●	
Bach's *Musette in D* 23				◆
Goodbye Song 30	■		●	
Lesson 8				
Hello Song 1	■		●	
Do Re Mi Tapping Song 19	■		●	
Mozart Mouse's Song 25	■	★	●	
Mexican Hat Dance 26			●	
Beethoven's *Symphony No. 5 in C Minor* 27				◆
Goodbye Song 30	■		●	

Index: Songs by Lesson (continued)

Sequential Musical Content (by Lesson)	Singing	Playing Instruments	Moving to Music	Listening to Music
Lesson 9				
Hello Song 💿1	■		●	
Mozart Mouse's Song 💿25	■	★	●	
Twinkle, Twinkle, Little Star (without CD)	■		●	
Mexican Hat Dance 💿26		★	●	◆
Goodbye Song 💿30	■		●	
Lesson 10				
Hello Song 💿1	■		●	
Do Re Mi Tapping Song 💿19	■		●	
The Itsy Bitsy Spider 💿7	■		●	
Johnny Works with One Hammer 💿20	■	★	●	
Mozart Mouse's Song 💿25	■	★	●	
The Old Gray Cat 💿14	■		●	
Racing Car 💿8	■		●	
Twinkle, Twinkle, Little Star 💿16	■	★	●	
Mozart's Variations on *Twinkle, Twinkle, Little Star* 💿17				◆
Goodbye Song 💿30	■		●	

Index: Songs by Title (Alphabetical)

Musical Content (by Title)	Lessons	Singing	Playing Instruments	Moving to Music	Listening to Music
Do Re Mi Tapping Song 19	6, 7, 8, 10	■		●	
Do You Know? 5	1	■			◆
Giant's Lullaby 10	3, 4			●	◆
Goodbye Song 30	All	■		●	
Hello Song 1	All	■		●	
High and Low Song 3	1, 2, 5, 10			●	◆
If You're Happy and You Know It 4	1, 2	■		●	
Itsy Bitsy Spider, The 7	2, 3, 10	■		●	◆
Johnny Works with One Hammer 20	6, 10	■	★	●	
Mexican Hat Dance 26	8, 9		★	●	◆
Mozart Mouse's Song 25	8, 9, 10	■	★	●	
Musette in D (Bach) 23	7				◆
Old Gray Cat, The 14	4, 5, 6, 10	■		●	◆
Racing Car 8	3, 4, 7, 10	■		●	
Rage Over the Lost Penny 11 (Beethoven)	3				◆
Stars and Stripes Forever (Sousa) 21	6			●	◆
Surprise Symphony (Haydn) 12	4				◆
Symphony No. 5 in C Minor 27 (Beethoven)	8				◆
Twinkle, Twinkle, Little Star 16	5, 9, 10	■	★	●	
Variations on Twinkle, Twinkle, Little Star (Mozart) 17	5, 10				◆

CD Credits

Producer: Alan Billingsley

Narrator: Janice Roper

Beethoven Bear: Connor Berkompas

Mozart Mouse: Julia Roper

Singers: Dana Cooper, Sarah Hammond, Karl Hampton, Sami James, Erin Johnson, Samantha Thomas, David Wilson

Orchestrations by Alan Billingsley except: *Stars and Stripes Forever* and Beethoven's *Fifth Symphony* licensed from *Network Music.*

Piano performances of *Rage Over the Lost Penny* and *Variations on Twinkle, Twinkle, Little Star* by Kim Newman.

CD Track List

Track	Title
1	*Hello Song*
2	Chapter 1 Story
3	*High and Low Song*
4	*If You're Happy and You Know It*
5	*Do You Know?*
6	Chapter 2 Story
7	*The Itsy Bitsy Spider*
8	*Racing Car*
9	Chapter 3 Story
10	*Giant's Lullaby*
11	Ludwig van Beethoven's *Rage Over the Lost Penny*
12	Franz Joseph Haydn's *Surprise Symphony*
13	Chapter 4 Story
14	*The Old Gray Cat*
15	Chapter 5 Story
16	*Twinkle, Twinkle, Little Star*
17	Wolfgang Amadeus Mozart's *Variations on Twinkle, Twinkle, Little Star*
18	Chapter 6 Story
19	*Do, Re, Mi Tapping Song*
20	*Johnny Works With One Hammer*
21	John Philip Sousa's *Stars and Stripes Forever*
22	Chapter 7 Story
23	Johann Sebastian Bach's *Musette in D*
24	Chapter 8 Story
25	*Mozart Mouse's Song*
26	*Mexican Hat Dance*
27	Ludwig van Beethoven's *Symphony No. 5 in C Minor*
28	Chapter 9 Story
29	Chapter 10 Story
30	*Goodbye Song*